being**Davina**

beingDavina

The biography of Britain's best-loved TV star

Nigel Goodall

JOHN BLAKE

Published by John Blake Publishing Ltd,
3, Bramber Court, 2 Bramber Road,
London W14 9PB, England

www.blake.co.uk

First published in hardback in 2006

ISBN 1 84454 246 7

British Library Cataloguing-in-Publication Data:

A catalogue record for this book is available from the British Library.

Design by www.envydesign.co.uk

Printed in Great Britain by Creative Print and Design, Wales

1 3 5 7 9 10 8 6 4 2

Papers used by John Blake Publishing are natural, recyclable products
made from wood grown in sustainable forests. The manufacturing processes
conform to the environmental regulations of the country of origin.

Pictures reproduced by kind permission of mirrorpix and Rex Features.

'I'm a complete slapper –
I work for any channel that'll pay me.'
Davina McCall

'For me, biography has always been a personal adventure of exploration and pursuit, a tracking. Like love, in passionate curiosity.'

– Richard Holmes, *Sidetracks: Explorations of a Romantic Biographer*

To my son Adam and his girlfriend Miya,
my daughter Kim; and for giving me a whole
new world, my grandson Harvey.

Also by Nigel Goodall:

Christian Slater: Back From the Edge

What's Eating Johnny Depp

Kylie Naked: A Biography
(with Jenny Stanley-Clarke)

Demi Moore: The Most Powerful Woman in Hollywood

The Ultimate Queen
(with Peter Lewry)

Winona Ryder: The Biography

The Ultimate Cliff
(with Peter Lewry)

Jump Up: The Rise of the Rolling Stones

George Michael: In His Own Words

The Complete Cliff Richard Chronicle
(with Peter Lewry)

Elton John: A Visual Documentary

Cher: In Her Own Words

Cliff Richard: The Complete Recording Sessions
(with Peter Lewry)

www.nigelgoodall.co.uk

CONTENTS

ACKNOWLEDGEMENTS

This book is also dedicated to the memory of Kate King, one of the most caring and kindest people you could ever wish to meet. Her untimely death from cancer, a few years ago, at such a young age, is a loss to all that knew her. During my early writing career, Kate transcribed many an interview for me, simply and unselfishly, to help me out. I will always cherish her friendship, love and care.

A big thanks to everybody who helped and encouraged me as this book took shape: my son and daughter, Adam and Kim, who are more excited about this book than any other I have done. Davina is one of their favourites after *EastEnders* Phil and Grant Mitchell (sorry, Davina!). To everybody at John Blake Publishing – especially my editor Mark Hanks, who also did a fabulous job with the picture sections; my copy editor, Jane Donovan, for everything she did for this book and all the hard work; my research team Keith Hayward, Kerry Peddar and Mark Barker, who all did me proud with the information they dug up; Neil Rees for his recollection of *God's Gift* and for guiding me to information on Kylie Minogue's *Word Is Out* music video; Melanie Beadon at 2 entertain for the Davina *30 Minute Workouts* DVD, which I promise to exercise with real soon, and to Elkie Brooks for sharing her thoughts with me about *Reborn In The USA*. I look forward to collaborating with you again on your biography. To Sean Delaney at the British Film Institute for his help with the television listing; Elizabeth Cunningham for the *Top Gear* tape and for the title of this book; Charlotte Rasmussen for your eagle eye, critique and for being such a huge fan of my previous works. Thanks, too, to Guy Buckland for the great photo of me on the jacket and for making me look like a real author! To Carol Hall for my website, and to my friends, Anne and Jan, for suggesting Davina would make a good book; and Mike and Caroline for you know why. We must try and not be so busy in future so that we can meet up more often. I would also like to mention the many excellent websites dedicated to all things *Big Brother*, particularly the Celebrity Big Brother UK Website (bigbrotherwebsite.net), which I consulted during my research. And last but not least, thanks to the Royal Literary Fund, who again provided me with funding so I could keep writing. Without them this book would simply not have been possible.

1

A CRY FOR HELP

Davina McCall was 15 years old when she turned up at school wearing black leather trousers and a T-shirt ripped across the waist. She had dyed her hair aubergine and was wearing Gothic make-up. It was 'mufti day' at Godolphin and Latymer School in Hammersmith, West London, and, while most girls came dressed like Bananarama wannabes in ra-ra skirts and legwarmers, Davina went punk.

Although in the spring of 1983 – the year Karen Carpenter died of anorexia nervosa, the eating disorder about to plague Davina – punk was probably no longer embraced by the mainstream. Punk dress and music were now considered wild, weird and antisocial, and the people who liked it weren't much better, but, for Davina, it was essential for the attention she craved. During the same year, she remembers she shaved her head because she was sick of people constantly saying she dyed her hair blonde to make herself look like Princess Diana: 'I was mortified because I was trying to be trendy and tough.'

It wasn't the first time that Davina had reinvented herself. Three years earlier, when punk was still in vogue, she was simply horrified when she arrived for her first day at school. 'I was this prim and proper little thing who turned up on her first day wearing white socks pulled up to her knees, a little A-line skirt, a Pringle haircut and was carrying a briefcase from WH Smith that pulled out like a doctor's case. And I walked in and saw everybody – there were all these punks and trendy types, it was a nightmare. They all had streaked hair and their socks were round their ankles, and they all had Millets bags with "The Sex Pistols" and "The Clash" written on them. I had never heard of those bands and I just thought, "I am going to die. Ground, eat me up, please!"

'But actually kids are brilliantly resilient and within three days I too had streaked my hair. And I went and got my bag from Millets – and wrote the names of bands I never heard of before on it – because I wanted desperately to fit in.' During this time she also recalls that she even changed the way she spoke when she got 'a bit of hassle' from some kids in Shepherds Bush on her way to school: 'So I started talking "loik vat" for survival because I thought I was going to be beaten up.

'It was like Sandra Dee from *Grease* turning into a wild Pink Lady! I never looked back really; it was like a rebirth. When my granny next saw me, she was most perturbed. An old school friend came round for dinner recently and we had such a laugh recalling my third day at school. She says she'll never forget it because I'd changed so dramatically. And since then I've been many people, and I like to play different parts of myself – sometimes a foxy minx, sometimes quiet and sensitive, sometimes loud and gregarious – and they're all me.' Basically, though, she continues, 'I am two people and they are incredibly different. There is the little girl who was brought up by my grandmother and who was taught very good morals and manners, and right from wrong. And then there is my French side, which I get from my mum and Paris – and going out and wild parties, and madness and excitement.'

It was after that third day at the school that she started experimenting with her looks – she had to. The easiest way to reinvent yourself, she says, 'is with your hair. It's immediate and it's shocking. I've had black hair, orange hair, blonde hair, and you get a lot of attention as a blonde. When I went dark again, I had to suddenly develop a sense of humour to get noticed – I had to work harder for it.'

Having learned from an early age that 'to get on you have to fit in' has probably helped Davina become one of Britain's most loved television presenters without the need for the kind of fame to be found from being crowned 'Queen of the Celebrity Jungle'. Or being an ex-Atomic Kitten, a member of Girls Aloud or a Sugababe. And fit in she still does, even with the way she talks. She has a sort of middle-class cockney twang to her accent that, according to journalist Paul Bracchi, places her somewhere roughly 30 miles up any motorway heading out of London. But, if the secret of success is an unsettled childhood, Davina was destined for greatness when she was just three years old and was sent off to live with her grandparents. Not because she was difficult or troublesome but because she was, to all intents and purposes, abandoned by her parents when they divorced in 1970.

Davina Lucy Pascale McCall was born on 16 October 1967 in Wimbledon, Southwest London, and was the only child of a French-born mother, Florence, and an English father, Andrew. Florence – who already had a daughter, Caroline, from her first marriage – was also very glamorous. By all accounts, according to Davina ('Div' for short), she was 'a wild sixties person who didn't have it in her to look after me. She was very young when she had me and I don't think she could cope with the responsibility of a child.' So she fled from the Yves St Laurent boutique she managed in Knightsbridge and ended up living in an apartment located in the exclusive 8th arrondissement in Paris, near the Champs Elysées.

What is curious, however, is how, if she couldn't cope with looking after Davina, she coped with bringing up Caroline, who had arrived in the world five years before. Florence would have been just 18 years old then, and surely having a child so young would have been far more daunting than having one at 23. But then again it was the decade of rebellion: a decade in which free thinking, free love and free drugs were the buzzwords of a generation. The burgeoning counterculture scene of two years earlier was now in full bloom and the entire world, it seemed, felt the need to go to San Francisco and put flowers in their hair. Just six months before Davina was born, Muhammad Ali refused to be drafted into the US Army to serve his national service as a protest against the war that continued to grind on in Vietnam, and, in the process, was stripped of his World Heavyweight Boxing Championship belt.

More peacefully perhaps, Elvis Presley married Priscilla Beaulieu in a secret ceremony in Las Vegas.

But even that could not be regarded as completely without hysteria when you consider that at that time the marriage of a pop star – and in this instance the biggest pop star of all– would have brought certain death to a colourful career. Despite a run of less than mediocre movies, Elvis was still clearly a heartthrob. Of course, there was more at stake than just a career. What would the world have thought to discover that Priscilla was barely 14 when plucked from a US Air Force base in Germany to become Elvis's child bride?

Whatever it was that caused Davina's mother to flee back to her native France, it would now be up to her father Andrew (who still calls her 'Divvy Poohs Pops' – and who Davina, who already had her mother's Gallic good looks, describes as 'the love of her life') to decide what would be best for her. Realising he would probably not cope that well with the emotional demands of bringing up a daughter on his own while trying to hold down his job as a sales rep for fashion house Jaeger, he thought a good option would be for Davina to live with his parents in Bramley, Surrey. At least then she would have some kind of stability in her life and, if nothing else, he could see her at weekends. But Sundays, Davina recalls, 'were full of dread because he had to leave'.

For Davina, it was perfect. She was, after all, very gung-ho, a bit of a tomboy, always building houses out of tree stumps, riding a lot and, overall, was very outdoorsy. In fact, it was because she was so outdoorsy that she would imagine she was the sixth member of Enid Blyton's *Famous Five*, the classic series of 21 children's adventures, published over 20 years from 1943. Even now, it is one of the most popular series of children's books in England and America, still selling over 2 million copies a year. She remembers, 'I'd go out with a quiver and arrows I'd made out of kitchen rolls and sticks, sit on the gate and wait for them to come and take me on an adventure.'

Interestingly enough, to this day the stories remain the favourite among the most enjoyed books that adults read as children. And from that point of view it is not difficult to understand why they would have been one of Davina's favourites as well. Like Louisa May Alcott's *Little Women*, Blyton's *Famous Five* was about family loyalties, bonding and friendship, something Davina may have thought was perhaps missing from her own early upbringing. And what is the point of reading children's fiction if not to make the unbelievable believable?

Although not in a book and still a few years away, Davina would soon have other favourites, such as television's popular sci-fi series *Star Trek*, the movie versions of which she still watches every Christmas. She also shared an obsession with all British and

American girlhood: *Starsky and Hutch* star Paul Michael Glaser. In fact, so obsessed was she with Glaser that she would never miss a single episode. But perhaps the strangest crush she confesses she had was on comedian Freddie Starr. 'It started when I was young, but I did fancy Freddie. I used to tell everyone I was going to marry either my dad or Freddie. I thought he was the funniest person ever. He used to do this thing where he walked into the microphone and hit his head. I thought it was absolutely hilarious.'

For the time being, though, and before falling for those who frequented our small screens, despite her parents going their separate ways when Davina was still an infant, 'it was like all my Christmases had come at once,' she raves. 'I was spoiled rotten. I had lovely granny food made for me all the time; she'd bake cakes and delicious treats. I still saw Mum in the holidays. Even though I missed her at first, I just got on with it, really.

'When you're that age and your life changes you don't really understand what's going on. All I know is that I had a lot of love. I had my grandparents spoiling me during the week, I saw my dad at weekends, and then jetted off to stay with Mum during the holidays.' At first, she says, 'my mum was a very exciting woman to be around, an electric personality. There was always a drama happening but she was always funny. She'd do the really embarrassing thing that you would never dare to do. I used to watch *Absolutely Fabulous* and I sometimes used to think, "Gosh, that's like me – I'm Saffy and my mum's Edina." Not the same kind of fashion preciousness, but that kind of relationship where she made me more square because I was constantly trying to look after my mum and keep her under control.'

But, if you asked her today how embarrassing her mother was, she would probably tell you, 'Well, I'm thinking of an electric-blue floor-length fake fur that made her look like Cruella De Vil, which she'd waft around in. And she'd go to a café and have a double Ricard before she went to work, and she'd be flirting with somebody, you know, inappropriate, and you'd be thinking, "Oh my God!" and she'd do citizen's arrests when someone pinched her bottom. Just mad stuff, but funny and fantastic... if you're not the daughter. My friends would say, "Oh my God, she's so cool." But I didn't tell people a lot of the stuff that happened in France and I especially didn't tell my English family because I didn't want to upset them, or for them to stop me going over there because I loved my mother.

'It was like having three families. For a while, I was the envy of all my friends. The main thing was I was loved. However, I'm sure I was also a bit confused by the unsettling aspects of living with three different sets of people. It wasn't until I was in my late twenties that I could put it into perspective. I actually realised what it was about, that I was very lucky to have had so much love. It's a lot worse for other children whose parents split up – I was treated like a goddess. Before then, though, I'd gone a bit wild, not surprisingly.'

In fact, it was only a couple of years ago that 'my granny and I were talking about memories from child-hood and I was remembering how I used to sit at the feet of my great-granny – who also lived with us – and how I would pinch the skin at the top of her hand and watch how long it would take to go back down again; and how she had these little things in her purse – like a pixie in a black cap – which she'd let me play with. And a couple of days later, my granny had gone through the house and found the little pixie and sent it to me in the post, and now I have it in my purse.

'That was very emotional for me... a memory from 35 years ago and she still had it, and now I've got it. And she's just done the most fantastic book for me, called *The Grandparents Book*, with all our family's stories and the treats she was allowed when she was a little girl. And our family tree from way, way before me, and it's these things that are really important to me, and will be even more so when she goes.'

With so much love, isn't it surprising that, by the

time she was 15, Davina was to struggle with the onslaught of anorexia nervosa? In 1994, it was one of the eating disorders afflicting 8 million sufferers in the United States, and in Britain at least 60,000 people were known to have been affected by it, but the actual figure was probably twice that.

So what exactly is anorexia nervosa? Is it a plain obstinacy in the form of a dieting obsession? Or a craving for the attention gained by a person's skeletal shape that would attract anyone who saw them? Or is it, as many theorise about sufferers, perhaps a deep-rooted psychological problem that is a blurred signal to a parent with whom there might be a relationship problem. In other words, is it a cry for help, one that can take on all forms of addiction, whether alcohol, drugs or anorexia?

Such addictions or just generally bad behaviour do seem to haunt celebrities when, at some time or another in their career, their public profile falls from grace. It's always the ones least likely to tarnish their reputations, too. Some would reason that is why Winona Ryder shoplifted thousands of dollars' worth of designer clothes and accessories from Saks Fifth Avenue in Beverly Hills in December 2001. At the time, the question on everyone's lips was why would anyone worth $30 million need to steal what she could easily buy. Many were convinced it was Ryder's cry for help.

But anorexia is a different story. It was, after all, what killed singer Karen Carpenter, who was the first celebrity to die after battling with the disorder for seven years. What is so strange about Karen's untimely death, however, is that she had no death wish. It was quite the opposite, in fact. She wanted to go on making music and expand her talent into other fields of entertainment throughout her life. If anything, Karen was a traditional showbusiness trouper. And yet anorexia seems to have been her cry for help. The question is, was it just an ugly and deadly equaliser for attention alongside her older brother, Richard, who was treated as the senior by their mother, and without whom Karen thought she would have no career? Or was it the fact that, because Karen never considered herself truly pretty enough to stand on a stage, starving was aimed at correcting her lack of self-esteem.

Whatever it was, according to Britain's *Concise Medical Dictionary*, 'anorexia nervosa is a psychological illness, most common in female adolescents, in which the patients have no desire to eat; eating may in fact be abhorrent to them. The problem often starts with a simple desire to lose weight, which then becomes an obsession. The result is a severe loss of weight and sometimes starvation. The underlying cause of the illness is complicated –

problems in the family and rejection of adult sexuality are often factors involved.'

Of course, Davina's fight with anorexia was less fateful than Karen Carpenter's and not so prolonged. It probably started when she felt she needed a hug and to be told she was loved – which sounds strange when you consider all the love she had showered on her from her 'three families'. But, according to her, it only lasted a couple of months and 'was a weird mixture of superbly confident and terribly insecure'.

In truth, as she admits herself, 'I was a troubled adolescent, who needed help and didn't know how to ask, so I did something radical to get noticed.' Perhaps more brutally, the reasons behind it may have been the all-too-familiar cocktail of teenage self-loathing and lack of self-worth. Certainly, says Davina, 'I thought I was ugly and fat. I missed my mum and felt confused, so I stopped eating for attention but more as a cry for help. Adolescence hit me hard. Suddenly, I couldn't talk to people, couldn't make myself understood – I was hurting.'

Isn't that what adolescence is all about, though? During the making of *Mermaids* in 1989, Winona Ryder would agree. It was a film she liked, 'because it shows the inconsistencies of being an adolescent – their sudden changes of mood'. That inconsistency is what she related to in her role as Cher's screen daughter, Charlotte Flax. 'One day she'll be obsessed with Catholicism, but the next day she'll be obsessed with Joe the gardener. And the next day she'll want to be an American Indian. I had really been going through stuff like that. I would think, "I'm going crazy! I don't know what I want! I don't know who I am." Sure, Charlotte's role was exaggerated,' she admits. 'But things are exaggerated at that age.' Winona saw Charlotte as 'the epitome of inconsistent teen angst'. She explains, 'You reach a point where you stop communicating because you can't articulate what you're feeling. You assume your parents can read your mind. You're confused, they're confused – it's a party of confusion.' And, of course, she was right. Wasn't that exactly what Davina was feeling and going through herself?

Although she was being treated like a goddess at home, at Bramley's St Catherine's Junior School near Guildford in Surrey, it was a different story entirely. That was when her troubles really began. Not that the school was to blame. In fact, there could not have been a better choice. Founded in 1885, by the time Davina enrolled there, the school had enjoyed over a century of tradition and already prided itself on its own very special blend of academic excellence and pastoral care. Certainly, as a girl's school, St Catherine's ensured that its students developed in an environment which made the girls believe that, whatever they did, there was nothing they could not achieve. Well, in Davina's case, that was certainly true...

All the same, 'I was given quite a hard time because I was so different; I got bullied and taunted about it,' remembers Davina. 'These girls sang little songs about me because I lived with my grandparents. And not having any money. It was a difficult time – I was teased mercilessly.' But overall she says she had a rosy childhood. Any child of her age would probably admit it sounded pretty idyllic, if you think about it – flitting between public school and London, France and holidays at plush ski resorts, such as Verbier, where she was spoiled rotten by her mother. While staying in France during her teens, she lost her virginity to a French boy. She remembers it as being totally unromantic. But having sex in a club's DJ booth some years later was better – well, sort of. As Davina explains, it happened while she was in charge of the music: 'I managed to carry on playing the records, though; it was so funny.'

Not so funny, and around the same time, was when she was caught peeing between two cars during a girls' night out. She was left mortified when one of the car's headlights came on, revealing her mid-pee. Davina cringed, 'I'd crouched down and started to pee when one of the cars switched its headlights on and began to move away. I was in mid-flow so I couldn't stop. It was night-time so at least it was dark, but nevertheless it was extremely embarrassing.'

By the time she returned to live with her father and his new wife Gaby in West London, she had turned 13, and was now enjoying a happy middle-class childhood and about to start a new school. This was when Gaby effectively became her mother and, according to Davina, 'never made me feel excluded'. She became much closer to her than she was to her own mother, who by October 2005 was on her fourth marriage and living in South Africa. Going home to live with her father, however, was when Davina's anorexic problems beckoned, and her weight reduced down from nine stone to a skeletal six.

It was only when a close friend spotted the problem and told her parents that 'they sat me down with a salad and said, "Eat it and let's talk" that the floodgates opened. They were more than willing to give me the support – I just had to ask. After that, I went back to eating normally. I was lucky because I haven't been dogged with it.'

In another, more elaborate telling, Davina recalls that, 'as soon as my dad and my stepmum realised I wasn't eating, they put a stop to it. They sat me down and had a really good chat. It was like a block; I needed someone to ask if I was all right and for me to tell them. I felt awful and let it all come out, which it did.' The only downside to it all, as she explains, was that 'my father worked hard to send me to a posh school, and there was never any money left over'.

That 'posh school', as she describes it, was the Godolphin and Latymer School in Hammersmith, West London, which was not only academically high achieving but also hip and fashionable. For someone like Davina, who could probably best be described at that time as a sweet country tomboy, it could have seemed quite a pressurised environment in which to be educated. Situated on a four-acre site with its own playing fields, the school was very conveniently placed just a five-minute walk from Hammersmith Broadway tube. Although several additions have been made to the original Victorian building since she attended, including a gymnasium, pottery room, computer suites and a language laboratory, it was then a school for 700 girls aged between 11 and 18.

Built in 1861 as the Godolphin School, a boarding establishment for boys, and set in fields near the River Thames at Hammersmith in 1905, it became an independent day school for girls, associated with the Latymer Foundation and taking the name of Godolphin and Latymer. One year later, it received grants for equipment, library books and buildings from the London County Council and the Board of

Education. By 1951, the school had Voluntary Aided Status under the 1944 Education Act, and in 1977, rather than becoming a non-selective school under the state system, it reverted to full independent status.

According to the school's internet website, it is an excellent place of learning that suffers an unfair comparison with the neighbouring St Paul's, but if your daughter goes there today she is as good as in university and, at the time of writing, it would cost you £3,490 per term. Today, the school has 707 girls from ages 10 to 19. Just a slight difference to when Davina was there, with such other famous pupils as Kate Beckinsale, Samantha Bond, Sophie Ellis Bextor and one of Davina's own classmates Nigella Lawson. But perhaps the most distinguished former pupil was Julie Tullis, who became the first British woman to attempt to scale Everest and to climb K2, the second highest mountain in the world and arguably the hardest.

Lawson, on the other hand, would probably have been someone Davina knew well. One of the UK's most influential food writers with a growing international reputation and several bestselling books to her name as well as the Channel 4 series *Nigella Bites*, she read Medieval and Modern Languages at Oxford. She went on to pursue a successful career in journalism, becoming deputy literary editor of the *Sunday Times*. With a successful freelance career writing for the *Guardian*, the *Daily Telegraph* and *The Times Magazine* in Britain, she was equally successful in the States with *Gourmet* and *Bon Appetit*.

Her love of cooking and food had begun at home, but soon became part of her working life when she started a restaurant guide in *The Spectator* and a food column for *Vogue* magazine. Her first book, *How To Eat*, was published to critical acclaim in 1998 and established her relaxed attitude to food and eating, won her a wide and dedicated audience, and was, in fact, the basis for her successful Channel 4 series. The second series, interestingly enough, was accompanied by a tie-in book of the same name, which stayed in the bestseller lists for several months and helped to take worldwide book sales past the 1.5 million mark.

In 2000, things got even better when Lawson introduced a whole new generation to the art of baking with another bestseller, ironically titled *How To Be A Domestic Goddess*, which in turn won her an Author of the Year nomination at the British Book Awards. Eight years earlier, she had married fellow journalist and broadcaster John Diamond, who was diagnosed with throat cancer in 1997 and died in 2001. Today, she lives in London with their two children, Cosima and Bruno, and her second husband, art collector and advertising guru Charles Saatchi.

Kate Beckinsale, of course, was six years younger, so

the likelihood of Davina knowing her is remote. Unlike Lawson and Davina, Beckinsale went on to scale the heights of Hollywood. Born on 26 July 1973, to Judy Loe and the late actor Richard Beckinsale, to this day she has spent most of her life in London. In 1991, she made her acting debut in a television World War II drama, *One Against the Wind*. It was after leaving Oxford University's New College, where she majored in French and Russian literature, that she knew she wanted to be an actress.

During her first year at Oxford, Beckinsale landed herself a role in Kenneth Branagh's big-screen adaptation of Shakespeare's *Much Ado About Nothing* (1993). She subsequently appeared in a few notable but low-profile films, including *Cold Comfort Farm* (1995), *Shooting Fish* (1997) and *The Last Days of Disco* (1998). Although her first major American film, *Brokedown Palace*, in 1999 almost went unnoticed, it was when she was cast in *Pearl Harbor*, one of the highest-grossing films of 2001, that Beckinsale found herself placed among *FHM*'s 100 sexiest women in the world and firmly in the frame for even greater success in such films as *Serendipity* (2001), *Underworld* (2003), *Van Helsing* (2004) and *The Aviator* (2004).

Even though school may have had its difficulties, remembers Davina, outside, 'I had so much love from my dad and my stepmum, and my mum and my grandparents, but, when I look back at myself, I'd just try and give myself a little cuddle. I don't think anything could change the situation; we all make the best of things – I think I was a bit of a lost kid more than anything else.'

Lost or not, not all the tokens of her teen years would be so easy to dispose of. The stylised alien based on the original 1979 movie creature tattooed on her bottom is one of them. It's not surprising she had it done in the first place when you consider that the film and its creature are still regarded as one of the benchmarks of modern science-fiction horror. In fact, not since the heyday of George Lucas's 1977 *Star Wars* trilogy had a movie burst so violently into the popular consciousness as *Alien* had in 1979. Even though the sheer horror of the original movie has long been dissipated by the alien's own appearance in comic books and toy stores, Davina still wanted it removed: for no other reason than she now simply hated it. Unlike the rose on her wrist that she had done when she was 18 and feeling worse for wear, or the horns engraved on each hip when she was in Los Angeles, the alien tattoo, 'just frightens the living daylights out of me'.

Perhaps to Davina, it has the same effect as if Frankenstein's monster had looked in the mirror.

Although the creature in the film was clearly a man in a suit, it was still enough to horrify. Based on the monster created by HR Giger for the movie, the tattoo sported a grotesque exterior resembling a cyborg turned inside out and an elongated head that was not so subtly phallic in nature. The double rows of teeth and back protrusions helped complete the sense of dread. In the end, though, Davina decided it would be less painful to leave it where it was, no matter how scary. So she kept it as a reminder of what she calls her misspent youth.

2
DANGEROUS ADDICTIONS

By the time Davina was 16, she had left school with nine O levels, two A levels and she could speak French fluently – certainly enough qualifications to follow her classmates into university. But, rather than do that, she decided she only wanted to think about finding fame as a rock singer. Of course, as she would soon discover, that wasn't so easy. It wasn't easy then, and it certainly isn't any easier now; if it was, then there would be no need for television talent shows like *Pop Stars* or *The X-Factor*. She may have been singing with a band while she was at school, but perhaps she now wondered whether that would bring her the kind of fame and fortune she so desired. Instead, she decided a good alternative would be a stint as a singing waitress at the Moulin Rouge in Paris, although *Hello* magazine reported that according to some sources she failed her audition.

The Moulin Rouge is still the most famous of all cabarets in the world. Since the beginning of the twentieth century, it has been one of the most legendary monuments of Paris. Edith Piaf, Yves Montand, Ginger Rogers, Lisa Minnelli and Frank Sinatra are just a few of the names to have played cabaret at the venue. It is also where topless dancers take audiences on a travelogue across the ages and continents with performances of folklore histories from all over the world. And of course it is the only place on earth where one can see the real French Can-Can.

Whether Davina failed her audition or not, by the time she returned home to London, she had already tried her hand at modelling, which still appears to be an almost traditional route chosen by many pretty young girls in their bid for fame and fortune. At first, it appeared to be a good way for her to get noticed, and there seemed no reason why she shouldn't succeed. She did, after all, have all the right criteria for what she thought was needed to become a successful model. What she hadn't counted on, perhaps, was that, strangely enough, she considered herself to be too short and fat for the catwalk. As she herself admits, 'I was the world's most unsuccessful model at 16.'

Perhaps she felt that, if she couldn't become a model herself, then she could help others who could. And so what would be better than to go and work as a booker for Models One, an agency in Covent Garden that had started up in 1968 with just three models on their books. Today, it is a very different story. Models One is one of the largest and most successful model agencies in Europe, and also one of the most respected in the world. And, as if to prove the point, they boast of being responsible for helping to build the careers of such models as Yasmin Le Bon, Jerry Hall, Greta Scacchi, Twiggy, Karen Elson, Gerard Smith, Charley Speed and Giles Curties – and they are probably right.

Models One wasn't the only job that Davina found herself. She was also taken on as a nightclub host and door greeter by a club in Notting Hill. Part of her job would include being at the club's entrance dressed in provocative outfits. On one night, it might be a sexy nurse's uniform, on another, a black leather basque with stockings and suspenders. The idea was to entice and select what the club owners considered the right type of risqué, but upmarket, clientele. With her day job at Models One then working at the club in the evenings, and later when she also had a spell as a disc jockey, it was very rare if her day ended much before three in the morning – and now, more often than not (and probably to keep herself going), in a drunken and drug-ravaged haze.

But, if that's what it took to become famous, then perhaps it's why she decided to also network her way around the London nightclub scene in the hope that she would get noticed. Although that is what eventually happened, according to some, it would – unbeknown to her father Andrew and Gaby – also introduce her to the cocaine, Ecstasy and heroin drug cults permeating 1980s London.

'I was a drug addict, a complete mess,' she openly confesses. Even though she admits to smoking cannabis when she was 14, 'my real problems began when I was 22 – you name it, I took it, although I never injected. It was all or nothing with me. I was a bright girl, but I wasted what should have been my golden years. It was a long time to be hooked on drugs and alcohol, and I definitely killed off a few brain cells. From 18 to 24, I went out clubbing a lot and took things to keep going. I had a job so I looked like I was holding everything together but then the cracks started to show. I began letting people down and turning up late for work. I was also starting to feel physically drained. Although it felt like I was having a great time, the drugs were ruining my life. Perhaps, she continues, it was 'just because everyone else was doing them, I thought I had to. It might have been fun at the beginning but it sure as hell wasn't fun after a while.'

Nor was it fun for anyone around her. According to one source from those times, who remembers her as a loud and colourful character, there was certainly a dark side to it all. She had basically plunged herself into a misspent but by no means wasted period of partying. 'She knew lots of people on the scene and was always out and about until late in the early hours. When she came into a room you immediately knew she was there. She used to wear very over-the-top clothes, fluffy coats and lots of red. She was very clubby. She had lots of energy and I think this is what attracted a lot of men to her – she certainly got a lot of attention from them. But I know she was very unhappy when she was doing drugs, even though she put on a great show that she was having a wonderful time, but even the brightest young things can't burn the candle at both ends forever.' With her hectic lifestyle of three hours' sleep a night, while holding down a full-time job, was it any wonder that things began to take their toll?

No, says Davina, but it was the control aspect that was so exhausting. 'It's like a white-knuckle thing – you know, trying really hard not to do something you really want to do, and you're constantly in your head thinking about the next time you can go and get some drugs.' She left a boyfriend whom she'd blamed for getting her into heroin, but, while he was able to quit, her habit got even worse. 'I realised, "Gosh, it's not his fault – I've got to look at me." And the last thing I wanted to do was stop taking everything. I just thought, "Am I still going to be a fun person to be around? And aren't I going to turn into a really boring person? And I don't want to be totally abstinent and I definitely can't do it for the rest of my life. You know, forget it." But I tried it every other way. I knew I had to cut things out, so I stopped taking heroin about two months before I got clean, but then I just had a major coke problem so I realised I'm obviously unable to take any drugs in moderation.'

Her relationships at the time weren't that much better. One of them was with Formula One racing driver Roland Ratzenberger, who was tragically killed while qualifying for the 1994 San Marino Grand Prix, the very same race that took the life of three-times world champion Ayrton Senna. Born in 1960 in Salzburg, Austria, Ratzenberger first shot to prominence by winning the prestigious Formula Ford Festival at Brands Hatch in 1986. After a further run of successes, and showing great promise in the European Formula 3 and Touring Car Championships, he won himself a successful career in the Japanese Formula 3000 series.

Picked from Japan to drive in the 1994 Formula One season for Nick Wirth's new Simtek team, he was perhaps an odd choice to many, even though he had already qualified in the Brazilian Grand Prix at Interlagos. What may have made him an 'odd choice' was the fact that he still had to make his F1 Grand Prix debut. He did that two weeks later at the Pacific Grand Prix in Japan, but it was while he was attempting to qualify for the third race of the season, in April of the same year, at the ill-fated Imola circuit that tragedy would strike. With a front-wing failure to his car, he ploughed all but head on into a concrete wall at almost 200mph at the Villeneuve kink. In doing so, he was to become not only the first driver to perish at a Grand Prix since 1982, but also the first since the deaths of Riccardo Paletti and Gilles Villeneuve, both on the same circuit.

His relationship with Davina, according to one friend, 'was very hush-hush at the time and I think initially it started out as an affair, but from what I can remember they may have even planned marriage eventually. She was devastated and it took her a long time to get over it.'

'Certainly,' said another of those ubiquitous 'friends', who always seem to be on hand to comment about showbiz affairs, 'she was well known on the London club scene, but it went beyond taking recreational drugs on Saturday night. Davina got sucked into this dangerous lifestyle. I knew she was taking heroin – not injecting, just smoking it. I saw her going into a dealer's house in Notting Hill on one occasion where she was going to get another fix. She was clearly hooked and had to fight very hard to pull herself out of it.'

Pulling herself out of it would be another matter entirely. For the time being she was quite happy to be seen at places like Taboo, the Camden Palace and Beetroot, which she used to haunt regularly and she knew most of the others who also frequented them, like Steve Strange, the late Leigh Bowery and, interestingly enough, Pete Burns, the former frontman and vocalist of new wave band Dead or Alive. He was most famous for their No. 1 single 'You Spin Me Round (Like A Record)' in 1985, and again when it was re-released in 2006, on the back of his newfound fame simply for being nasty on *Celebrity Big Brother*. 'I'd always quite cherished his kind of brutal honesty,' says Davina, describing the night when he started his bullying attack on *Baywatch* star Traci Bingham. 'But I have to say that Pete should not drink because, when he has a drink inside him, he becomes vicious and he was drunk that night.'

Steve Strange was, according to one internet site, 'the late 1980s seminal clubland king'. Perhaps more accurately, Strange would best be described as Newport's first official punk rocker. After organising a few local punk gigs in Wales, one of which resulted in a night of passion with Stranglers' bassist Jean Jacques Burnel, he moved to London in 1976, where he took speed and mingled with the likes of Billy Idol, Vivienne Westwood and Boy George.

Bored with punk, he and Rusty Egan set about creating their own more glamorous 'New Romantic' scene or, as he modestly calls it, the 'leisure revolution'. An appearance in David Bowie's *Ashes to Ashes* video was swiftly followed by hit records of his own with Visage. With 'a lethal cocktail of success and drug abuse', he soon became known for being both demanding and difficult, none more so than when Midge Ure walked out of the group after Strange insisted on riding down New York's Fifth Avenue on a camel to promote their American tour. The hits and the money dried up, and Strange went from supping champagne and snorting cocaine with celebrities to a far less glamorous existence.

Leigh Bowery, on the other hand, was far more complex than Strange. Following his arrival in London from Melbourne, Australia in 1980, he had a colourful exhibitionist career. He first made a name for himself for being an extraordinarily gay performer. His dramatic performances of dance, music and simple exhibitionism, while wearing bizarre and very original outfits of his own design, could be frequently seen in Taboo, the same nightclub in Leicester Square that Davina was to haunt. A large man, he used his costumes to exaggerate his size, and the effects were frequently overpowering for those who encountered him, and more so because of his confrontational style.

In the late 1980s, when Davina would have known him, Bowery collaborated as a dancer with the post-punk ballet dancer Michael Clark, having been the costume-designer for a number of years. He also participated in multi-media events like *I Am Curious, Orange* and the play *Hey, Luciani*, with Mark E. Smith and The Fall. In 1993, he formed *Raw Sewage* with Sheila Tequila and Stella Stein, and performed in 18-inch platforms at the *Love Ball* in Amsterdam, but the collaboration ended in dramas. Bowery went on to appear as Madame Garbo in *The Homosexual* or *The Difficulty of Sexpressing Oneself* by Copi at Bagleys Warehouse in London's King's Cross. In May 1994, he married his long-term female companion, Nicola Batemanin, just seven months before his death from an AIDS-related illness at University College Hospital in London on New Year's Eve.

Despite the fact that it has been reported elsewhere that it wasn't until 1997 that Davina was able to rid herself of the destructive legacy of addiction to vodka and any class A drug she could get her hands on through counselling, it was actually six years before. In 1991, her half-sister Millie came home and caught her under a duvet in the middle of the afternoon. At the time, Millie was 11 years old, and, according to Davina, could see right through her. 'She just looked at me and said, "Davina, you look awful!" And I thought, "God, you're right. What am I doing to myself?" I realised then I wasn't just harming myself, but I was letting other people down a lot.' Part of that 'letting other people down', Davina explained, was when 'I would tell Millie I would pick her up from school and just wouldn't turn up. She would have to make her own way home. I'm deeply ashamed of the way I treated my family.'

Not that she has any regrets today, or is about to apologise or be ashamed about what some may consider irresponsible behaviour. In fact, she is glad of the experience because of what it taught her. 'Without wanting to say, "Hey everybody, go and get a drug problem!" – which is definitely not what I am trying to say – I'd say to anyone thinking of taking drugs, "It's not cool, and it can ruin lives." I am grateful that I have been where I have been because it has definitely made me a more grounded person. It has given me gratitude. When you get clean, you get so grateful for the smallest bit of good news, and people's attitudes towards you change: you get asked to people's houses again, and you are asked out to dinner because you are no longer a pain in the arse.'

But now, as patron of Focus, a treatment centre for addicts in Suffolk run by Chip Somers, the person who gave Davina the most help when she needed it, she has – she says – been able to give something back: 'They treat people irrespective of income, which is really important because by the time someone is ready to ask for help they are not going to have the money – they will have spent it all on drugs.'

Although Millie was the initial trigger in Davina cleaning up her act, another turning point came when her best friend Sarah threatened never to talk to her again unless she turned over a new leaf. 'She gave me a real rollicking and told me I was a loser. I burst into tears and that's when my life started, when I stopped taking the drugs.'

Today, she still attends Narcotics Anonymous meetings: 'I have to be vigilant because I'll never stop being an addict even though I have been clean for [15] years. Different people do different things and that's what I do, and I love it. I feel very safe there because, if I get wellied, my willpower goes out the window. If I was drunk and someone went, "Do you want a line?" I can't guarantee that I would have the wherewithal to say no. In the summer I'm like, "Please, please,

I'm desperate for a chilled rosé" or in the winter a mulled wine.'

She says the reason she couldn't allow herself to have even one glass of wine – although her husband, Matthew Robertson, is a 'wine nut, who spends a lot of time doing that lovely ritual of decanting and sniffing, and swooshing, and sometimes, you think, "You know, it looks fun"' – is that she knows she's not the sort of person who can do 'one' of anything. Not that she was ever a double-whisky-first-thing-in-the-morning type of person: 'But it was doing my head in. Every day I felt like I'd been run over by a 10-ton truck. I'm an addictive person; I'm very driven but I can also be focused in a negative way, which was how I was to drinking. It took me a day to give up. It was affecting my life, so I just stopped.'

But, she continues, 'I would trust my life to an addict, an ex-addict who's working some kind of programme in their life, like a 12-step programme. I would trust them with my biggest secret, my life, because there's an unwritten code that makes them the most trustworthy person in the world. However, if an addict has used for one day, if I'd used for one day, I'd be the most manipulative untrustworthy person you could ever meet. Give me one drug and I'll just be your worst nightmare, and that's why I know I can't do it. In my mad heady days when I was younger – clubbing and all that – I was having a really good time and then it all got out of control. And the older I get, the more accepting I am that I'm going to change all the time but my core – my morals and my manners – will stay the same. Even when I was using drugs I was quite a moral person; I had good manners, like "Please could I have the class A drugs?" and I was quite a loving person.' But, of course, it could have turned out very differently indeed, if it was not also for the cautious counsel of one of her father's closest friends.

Andrew, who by now, in Davina's words, was 'a gorgeous graphic designer', was mates with Eric Clapton, who was also an old friend of Davina's aunt, and who better to help than someone who had actually had the same problem. No stranger to alcohol and drug addiction, it was Clapton who convinced Davina to check into a rehab centre in East Anglia. She did that as well.

Clapton's close friendship with Andrew was perhaps not the only reason why he wanted to help. Some years before her drug problem came out into the open, he and Davina had been romantically involved with each other for nine months. She was 18 and he was 41. Had she been as famous then as she is now, one can only imagine what the tabloids would have made of it. No doubt it would have been a relationship made in tabloid heaven. And had Clapton gone public about his mixed-up feelings about sex back then, announcing how he had in the past often used sex to bolster his low self-esteem, it would have been headline news. Although today he has changed his attitude towards women, there was a time, he says, when 'girlfriends became a way of avoiding being with myself. I'd see a woman in a room and I'd be magnetised, and usually that would be dangerous because I don't think you can be any good to anybody unless you're OK on your own.'

Similarly to Davina, Clapton was also raised by grandparents in Surrey. If, like her, the secret formula for success is an unconventional childhood, then again it is no surprise that Clapton – born out of wedlock and abandoned by his parents – would go on to become one of the most respected and influential artists from the 1960s rock era, and one of the very few to be a three-time inductee into the Rock and Roll Hall of Fame. Still widely regarded as one of the greatest and most influential guitarists in pop music history, his musical style has gone through multiple changes during a career that now spans more than 40 years. Although always faithful to his love of the blues, Clapton is perhaps also now seen as an innovator of the different musical genres that have taken his career from the blues to psychedelic rock, pop and reggae with such bands as John Mayall and the Bluesbreakers, the Yardbirds, Cream, and of course as a solo artist.

He first ran into trouble with drugs in the early seventies at a time when he was emotionally and professionally distraught with an unsuccessful solo album and an infatuation with Patti Harrison, the wife of his friend Beatle George Harrison. Although he would at one point even pawn his guitars to feed his heroin habit, Clapton eventually bounced back in the early eighties with a couple of hit albums and singles after a two-year hiatus. He finally won the heart of Patti Harrison – and not so happily ended up with a new addiction, this time to alcohol.

Bearing in mind that he probably came closer to a more fatal end than just another drink or another bout of drugs he was very well placed indeed to help counsel Davina about the same addictions with which he himself had battled. And with his music-biz background, he seemed the perfect mentor to help Davina in her bid to launch herself as a singer, and cut some demos with her at the Townhouse Studios in London during the summer of 1988. Although not much studio paperwork exists for the sessions, only one of the three tracks – 'I'm Too Good For You', recorded during a 10-day period and co-produced with Rob Fraboni – has since surfaced. But not on an official album: a bootleg titled *The Best Unreleased Session Album In The World Ever*, and it also appears on another five-disc collection called *Rare Unreleased Trax*.

But then again, as Davina admits, if her voice wasn't distinctive enough, what chance did she have of making it as a singer? Her voice just wasn't right, she says. 'I can roughly sing in tune but, to be absolutely honest, my voice was by no means different enough to warrant being a singer. One of the great things about Celine Dion – love her or loathe her – is that you know who it is the minute you hear her – same with Mariah Carey or Joss Stone. They've got a really distinctive sound, and that's what I didn't have.' And, with the other two tracks she recorded with Clapton, 'The Very Last Time' and 'Sticky Situation' still unreleased, not even on a bootleg, perhaps she was right.

So, if you were Davina, and had failed to launch yourself into a music career, wouldn't you be over the moon if you were recruited as a dancer for the then latest Kylie Minogue video? Of course you would. And that was something Davina managed to pull off three years after she had cut her demos with Clapton. It was not surprising that she was excited. Kylie had burst on to the UK music scene in 1988, having scored the biggest-selling single ever in Australia the previous year with 'Locomotion', and, over the next five years, she would become one of the most successful female recording artists of all time, out-selling and out-surviving almost every one of her contemporaries in much the same way as she does today.

Like Davina, at the time Kylie was also a regular fixture in the London clubs, so it should not come as any surprise that it would only be a matter of time before the two met. For Kylie, though, what mattered most is what she wore and why it was suddenly being talked about when previously not many would have given it a second thought. It's true, confirms Kylie. 'I was immersing myself in clubland culture and would dance at Subterania, among other places, in my slashed John Galliano skirt, until the place closed. It was more than just going down to the local disco; I felt that I lived in London and was part of it, and being influenced by the music and fashion coming out of it.' Certainly, it was a time when DJs, designers, photographers and stylists all assumed a new importance in the world of pop and fashion.

In fact, it was here, at Subterania in West London's Ladbroke Grove, where, according to rumour, Kylie would dance the night away with a huge entourage and at one time even get her foot stuck in a toilet. But, more importantly, it was also where she first met Davina, who was the door girl at the club, and that, according to some, is how she ended up in the video alongside another one of Kylie's then new friends, photographer Mario Sorrenti, also a regular at the club.

But not everyone would applaud her 'Word Is Out' single and the accompanying video. One of those was Kylie's own record producer Pete Waterman, who, by August 1991 when the single was released, felt that Kylie was no longer interested in making pop records for her public but for herself instead. But, as far as Waterman was concerned, what illustrated this was this single and the video that went with it. In the video, shot outside the PWL studios in London late at night, Kylie, in her slashed John Galliano skirt, black stockings and suspenders, portrayed herself as a prostitute and Davina played one of her sidekicks. Waterman had only been involved with the videos Kylie made for her first five singles or so, after which it was completely up to her what she wanted to do, but, to this day, he makes no bones about the reservations he held about the video. 'Dressing up as a prostitute wouldn't have been my choice and the public seemed to understand that as well because, once they saw it, her popularity just fell away.'

That, however, was several years after Davina had landed herself a job with MTV Europe, the music-based cable channel launched in Britain almost five years before 'Word Is Out' was released. As if to confirm Waterman's comments, 'Word Is Out' would become Kylie's first single not to reach the Top 10. Although Davina was said to have been talent-spotted, Eric Clapton could be said to be partially responsible for her MTV job. It was literally six months after she had stopped all the drugs and drink that, with his guidance, she bombarded the channel with phone calls, letters and showreels until they relented and gave her a presenting job on the midnight to 2am graveyard shift.

But then again it probably helped that she was ambitious to get on TV in the first place. She was really proud of herself when she finally got her opening: 'I spent three years just chewing at people's heels and annoying people – tenacious, addict without the drugs. Because the minute I put down the drugs, I needed something else to get my teeth into.' And not only that, she continues, 'but if I work at something half as hard as I used to work on scoring drugs – and addicts spend a lot of time and effort trying to maintain their habit – then I'm going to be extremely successful.' And that is exactly what she did.

3

GOD'S GIFT

By the time Davina joined *MTV's Most Wanted* as a
guest presenter in 1992, the Europe division of the
American cable channel had firmly established itself
as a full service network, and the biggest threat yet to
terrestrial television. Offering news, sports, sitcoms,
documentaries, cartoons, game shows and other
traditional television fare, the channel was building
on its own reputation of being by far the most
important outlet for music video programming.

According to Robert Thompson, professor of media
and popular culture, and the founding director of the
Center for the Study of Popular Television at Syracuse
University in New York, MTV is 'the only television
entity of any kind that ever had a generation named

after it. We don't even have the CNN generation, but we have the MTV generation. This came out as the centre of the universe for the demographic of young people and it managed to bring together people who would have been very disparate in what radio stations they listened to. But they all came together in this one television hangout.'

Perhaps most impressive about MTV was just how quickly it caught hold of youthful psyches in the early 1980s. It seems that, as suddenly as the appearance of the Rubik's Cube, a line was drawn in the schoolyard sand. Either you had seen the new Go-Go's video on MTV, or you were one of those who didn't have cable television. *TV Guide* journalist Jennifer Graham agrees: 'I was really, really into it. It was such a huge event, everyone was talking about it. It defined pop culture for us at that time.'

Certainly, many in the entertainment industry refer to those younger than 20 as 'MTV babies', because the station had such a major impact and influence on the way television programmes were then produced, and still are today. If nothing else, MTV was the one network that pioneered and introduced the fast-paced 'in your face' style of programming and advertising with quick cuts, layered graphics, multiple messages, loud audios, high-impact visuals, frenetic bursts and random transitions. Not before or since has there been a style that has affected a generation so much and its programming of every media type.

So is it any wonder that it was Davina's dream to work for the network while its success was still growing in Europe, or that she saw it as the perfect medium to launch herself into the world of television presenting? Not that she was in any rush to quit her job at Models One quite yet. She was only too aware that if everything was to go pear-shaped in her bid for fame, she would at least have a job to fall back on. The annals of television are littered with corpses of would-be star presenters who on any one day can wake up to the news that they have been dropped and replaced in favour of another new face. Even the lists of the ones who have in the past successfully moved from radio to television and then disappeared were endless.

Sixties DJ Simon Dee was perhaps the prime example of such success turned sour. Dee, one of the first voices of British offshore radio, joined Radio Caroline in 1964. One year later, he was the first pirate broadcaster to become a national star when the BBC offered him a show on the Light Programme. As well as his radio programme, he had a flourishing TV career and his Saturday-evening BBC chat show *Dee Time* was an enormous success. For a time he could do no wrong. But, by the end of 1970, after London Weekend

Television prematurely terminated his contract just a few months into his late-night chat show, his position as the media golden boy faded into oblivion.

Not that Davina was about to be put off by such tales of woe. 'I got on the show by purely persevering. It was my first big break and they put me on in the middle of the night so I could make loads of mistakes. They kept pulling me into the office and saying, "Calm down, you've got the job now!" But I was eager to please so they couldn't shut me up. I was like a coiled spring. I found it was my niche and that's what I really enjoyed, but being confident in front of an audience is something I've had to learn.'

Another DJ, John Barry, from the 1960s club scene, would agree with that summation. 'I must have been about 16 at the time and had just started going out to discotheques (as they were called then). And, in every one I went to, there was a disc jockey from one of the offshore pirate radio stations, and it kind of hit me: "Wow, these guys are really popular!" And on top of that I was also listening to stations like Radio London and Caroline 24/7, so I was pretty much influenced by the jocks of the day, like Johnnie Walker, Roger "Twiggy" Day, Dave Cash and, a bit later, Emperor Rosco, and to the music they were playing on air. So I decided that was what I wanted to do.

'What could be better, I thought, than having a job where you just play your favourite records and chat about them, and get paid for it? So I practised at home in my bedroom, with a small record deck, just playing the first couple of seconds of each record, taking it off, putting another on, or the same one back on again and was also doing the in-between record chat, over and over, using a hairbrush as a microphone in front of a mirror till I got it to sound and look right.

'Next step was to march into a club and ask if they needed a DJ. No, they didn't – but I kept going back to pester until they finally agreed to let me do a 20 or 30-minute spot two evenings a week as the punters came in. Although I wasn't allowed to use the mike and wasn't allowed to talk the record in, it was a start. So there I was just changing the records until the regular guy took over. And, for doing that, I got as much free Coca-Cola as I could drink in an evening!

'So, after a few weeks of just putting the records on, I started to nag the club to let me talk the records in and, finally, after much debate, they relented and let me have a go one evening. And, as you do, I made a bunch of mistakes – silly things like having the mike switched to off for the first disc I played, getting tongue twisted on another, putting the wrong side of a record on, and so on. So don't think I made much of an impression that first time. But the club was very gracious and gave me another try, and another, till I got it right!

'And when I did get it right, it was great. Being allowed to introduce each record, well, wow, it was what I wanted and a great first experience of how to be and react with a live audience. But it was only because I persevered, probably to the point of annoying, that the club finally gave in, but it meant I got the experience that all first-timers need, whether club, radio or television.'

Of course, gaining experience for presenting on television was a lot more difficult than getting experience as a DJ in a club. You couldn't just walk into a TV station and ask if you could have a go at it. Barry started out as a disc jockey in an era when the clubs and pirate radio stations were overcrowded with those keen enough to get seasick or drink as much Coke as they could in an evening. Although Davina would use the same perseverance as John Barry to get her first experience, it wasn't as if fame knocked at her door, or was delivered to her on a plate. If she was going to succeed, then she was literally going to have to bombard MTV with letters, phone calls and tapes. She is said to have done that for three months until they relented, took her applications seriously and offered her the opportunity she had dreamed of.

Most Wanted, it seemed, was an ideal showcase for

the innovative open style of presenting Davina had in mind. It was much the same as the other presenters on the show – Ray Cokes, Naughty Nina and Andy Cam – had adopted as well. The show aired every Tuesday to Friday evening and, according to many, its biggest appeal was that it offered viewer interaction, funny jokes, live music, famous guests and crazy competitions. Though some may have been dismissive of the show, by the time it ended (four years after it began), it had an unprecedented huge fan following. Strangely enough, MTV had decided to call it a day while it was still one of the most popular shows on the network, attracting some 60 million viewers across 38 European countries.

Aired live from the MTV headquarters in London, the show was, without question, an amazing achievement for a programme that had started out with a very economic budget and a very simple idea to simply entertain with zany, wacky and off-the-wall entertainment. On top of the weekday broadcasts, there were the occasional *Most Wanted* weekends, which started in the second year of the show's run with guests all very much in the musical mainstream and to the taste of the time. These ranged from Sting, Right Said Fred, Shane McGowan and Nick Cave to Crowded House, Take That and Björk. As with most television weekenders, *Most Wanted* was no different in coming up with ideas to grab as many viewers as they could and have them literally glued to their set from Saturday morning through till Sunday evening.

On one weekend, for instance, they set up cameras in two Hard Rock Cafés and had Davina, who now favoured striped jumpers worn with black miniskirts, coming live from Camden Market on the Saturday, and on the Sunday live from a fan's home in Germany. And, in the run-up to the last series, Wicked Will (who would go on to become a star in his own right with Chris Evans on *TFI Friday*) took the show to a new level of madness with items such as 'Live Public Club Bed', 'Devil Ray', 'Internet Ray Chat', 'Clean Our Souls' and 'Underwear Everywhere'.

To many a reader this must sound totally bizarre, but if you grew up in the MTV era then it was, as one viewer raved, 'a truly wonderful gem'. After years of tried and tested terrestrial television programming, one can understand why many considered it the greatest show on television. Nowhere was that more evident than when the kids arrived at school the next morning. Soon after they tumbled out of their parents' cars or the school bus, *Most Wanted* was the talk of the playground, where almost everyone simply raved about it. Much the same as it was in Davina's day when entire classes couldn't stop talking about the latest episode of *Star Trek* or *Starsky and Hutch*, or others would quote their favourite *Monty Python* sketches that had them in stitches the night before. Whereas Davina had probably raved about William Shatner, Paul Michael Glaser or John Cleese, now it was Davina and co from *Most Wanted* who were being raved about.

What is perhaps also interesting to note is how none of the other presenters from *Most Wanted* found the same enviable, almost unique level of success that Davina has. According to one journalist, it is her bright, brisk and bouncy personality that is just perfectly suited for presenting the kind of shows she hosts. But to Davina it was simply where she learned her craft. 'Generally speaking, I got on very well with everyone because I like people. Most American stars thought I was bonkers because female presenters in America are all the same – thin, beautiful, nip-tucked. I pull faces and say silly things, and they found it disarming to be interviewed by a dingbat,' she jokes.

If anyone could find a niche in television so reputably, then that person has to be Davina. She is, most agree, the one celebrity you can imagine having a good old gossip with over a glass of wine. Friend and confidante Jackie Clune would certainly agree. Not only does she confess to being a big Davina fan on a personal as well as professional level, but 'I've known her for several years. We worked on a programme called *Good Stuff* back in the 1990s and, although we haven't always stayed in touch, the minute she found out I was expecting triplets, she rang me to say she was sending me a maternity nurse as a present.'

The most memorable times that Clune remembers about Davina, however, are quite different to the glamorous, mature woman she has now become. These were the moments when 'we did a silly piece about male strippers and walked out of shot with our skirts hitched up and loo roll tucked into our knickers, or the time she let me tong her hair à la Farrah Fawcett for a piece about chicks with flicks. Or, more recently, the day I arrived at her house to find her in pigtails and dungarees, a child on each perfectly toned hip, laughingly trying to pass off a just-cooked fish pie as her own work.'

It is a far cry from when Davina was an almost total unknown at MTV and was then beginning to familiarise herself with the technical side of television, as well as learning a great deal about dealing with people and the public. Most of her time on *Most Wanted*, she says, was more or less spent 'just out on the street with roaming cameras and no audiences in sight'. But perhaps that was her greatest strength as a presenter, and still is. Looking back over her career today, it seems that is how she has spent most of it, and perhaps that is what makes her so popular with the public. She is, after all, one of the few presenters who can adapt to any situation in or out of a studio, with more ease than most.

As if to prove that point, by the time *Most Wanted* reached its final broadcast on 15 December 1995, Davina had already been recruited to present the first series of *God's Gift* for Granada Television, but not many critics were convinced about it. Despite it being classed as an X-rated version of *Blind Date*, the television reviewer writing for *Gay Times* was unimpressed: 'There has been a rapid sprouting of these cheap, cheesy lonely heart shows.' At the time BBC2 had *Singled Out*, an MTV buy-in, while ex-Capital Breakfast DJ Chris Tarrant was hosting *Man O'Man* featuring 10 pieces of male eye candy and 200 overexcited women.

In an attempt to vary things, the queer card was played with four alternative shows. Budgets may have been tight because the opening titles, in which a yellow-painted man sporting vine leaves on his lower half is ogled by numerous leather-clad women, remained the same. At least Davina got off lightly, being described as 'the miraculous, mouth-watering Davina McCall'. In each show five contestants are set six tests of manliness. In between all this (and similarly to the voice of *Big Brother*), there's a 'Voice of God' played by Stuart Hall (*It's a Knockout*) in his own inimitable style.

One particular show featured black aerobics instructor Gary, who was 'shitting himself' despite his 45-inch chest; recruitment consultant Jonathan from Salford, who claimed an inside leg of 35 inches 'with a built-in extension'; James from London, a blue-eyed stunner, Crusaid volunteer and an apparent descendant of Richard Lionheart; the voluptuous drag artiste Dusty 'O', who was 25 years of age, and Nick, 'equerry to the royalty of Blackpool'. Each time the show's audience proved to be an extremely lively bunch, eager to participate in the six rounds designed to separate the Gods from the Geeks. 'Anything could happen on this most abnormal of nights,' accurately predicted Mr Hall.

The first round was 'Stud-U-Like', which gauged the essential ingredient of sex appeal. Eager to prove himself, Gary couldn't wait to strip off in a laundry, juddering his butt against the machine ('It's fucking gorgeous!'), meanwhile Jonathan had a play with a shower and Dusty was given the job of vacuuming a rug from IKEA. The hapless contestants' chat-up lines were then put under the microscope with 'Smarm or Charm'. Witticisms varied from the jaded 'Do you come 'ere often?' to 'Do you fancy a bit of this succulent bird?' and 'Is that potted meat or jellied roll?'

Still more nauseous, and surely enough to get phones ringing constantly at the Duty Office, was 'Suck It and See', an exercise in which the lads' sensuous streak was checked out when they had to caress tummy-buttons with their tongues. Mucky faces wiped, the 'dirty rotten rats' were happy to dish the dirt 'Dish in the Dock', mostly to get their revenge on ex-lovers who slept around. One man had scrubbed a lavatory using his lover's toothbrush, while another faxed compromising pictures of his unfaithful beau to the office. Worst of all was the man who told his boyfriend that his father had just died so that he could have sex with someone he'd just met in a club.

So desperate were these guys for a date they even did a 30-second party piece ('Larf or Barf') featuring a fertility frolic, pelvic squats, saucy comedic talent and a puppet show. It was so bad that four men were booed off stage, while the audience was wowed by the talents of Dusty 'O' singing her hit song 'Glamour State of Mind' (available on Pushka Records). 'It just goes to prove,' she said, 'queens do have fabulous taste.'

'Bare Essentials' was a real test of machismo, in which homo-mortals stripped to their smalls in a last-ditch, 15-second chance to beat off the competition. Gary unsuccessfully sucked in his beer belly, Dusty gave us a glimpse of her pink gingham bikini, and the rest revealed a dreary collection of Calvin Klein-style briefs, with gratuitous bum shots galore. Over tumultuous cat-calls, Davina quickly responded to events by yelling, 'That was the quickest undressing ever!' So how did the audience choose their Gay God's Gift? They pushed hankies into the contestants' briefs. Nice! Ultimately, Nick was the chosen one, winning a purple sash, a tacky crown and a dinner date with a member of the audience.

The *Gay Times* reviewer felt sufficiently inspired to write, 'I'm swithering as to whether *Carnal Knowledge* and *God's Gift* are just affable programming or simply vacuous schedule fillers'. He went on to say, 'I can't seriously believe that TV companies think they're offering a reasonable alternative to a gay viewing audience as I'm positive lesbians and gays would demand something a little less cretinous, even in addition to programmes like these. I know I have a reputation as a crabby old critic and that maybe I should chill out – after all, it's all fun, isn't it? OK. I'm safe.' He finished by warning his readers, 'don't come running to me in five years' time when your brains have all rotted from watching this sort of show.'

But, according to fans of the show, yes, it was slightly embarrassing but fun at the same time. Why wouldn't it be? Never before had a programme focused on five lads who really fancy themselves and try to persuade an audience of randy drunken women (or, sometimes, gay men) which ones they really want to have sex with. And where else could you see a succession of quiz rounds that see the men show off their limited talents in several different areas while Stuart Hall maniacally eggs them on with his voiceover? And where else on British television could you see a final round of a game show that has contestants stripping down to their underwear, while the women vote as to which lad is the winner, and who then picks a woman of his choice from the audience?

Sure, no one can dispute that the tasks of a game show wouldn't usually involve stuff such as licking cream out of a woman's belly-button, or sucking her toes, men dressing up as women to prove they could laugh at themselves, singing, dancing, serenading and being romantic. As one viewer from the time recalls, 'It was the first time I had seen Davina, and she was so loud and outrageous I thought she was a drag queen for a few seconds! But she was also perfect for the show though, and, when it came back for a second series with Claudia Winkleman presenting instead, it just went downhill because, compared to Davina, she wasn't anywhere near as cool. I seem to remember the first show had Davina in a bright-pink PVC skirt and jacket, and one memorable moment when one contestant stripped down to a G-string, and started wiggling his bum at the crowd, only for the crowd –

and Davina – to notice that he had some of his own excrement sticking out the back of his G-string!'

Looking back, would Davina agree with either of those summations? Probably not, but she does recall some of the letters she received from both sexes while working on the show. 'Women think I'm really funny. And the men always started off, "I'd never normally do this, but..." My favourite was from a 76-year-old lady who told me what she would do to my *God's Gift* assistant Glenn, if she were younger. I thought, "Great! I must be broadening my appeal."'

Although Davina claims *God's Gift* (one of her favourite shows) was her first adventure into television with an audience, the audience were, she shudders, 'all so drunk they were just going to clap and cheer whatever I said'. But, as most critics would agree, she had the flair to steer the show out of its potential doldrums. And it was that knack that was to land her another show, this time with a much higher profile, and one that would place her firmly on the television map. It was as if she has this fantastic timing, as if she instinctively knows the good decisions for her to forward her career. And perhaps 'instinct' remains the quality that best describes Davina McCall's choice of what shows to present. There were, however, some other obstacles to overcome before she could get where she wanted.

4

SNAKES & LADDERS

Davina had always wanted to be married by the time she was 30, and just weeks before her thirtieth birthday, in September 1997, her wish came true when she married part-time actor and wannabe vicar Andrew Leggett. The couple had met just six months earlier, in March of that year, at the Holy Innocents Church in West London.

Although religion and God, she says, is an inside job in all of us, Davina still prays regularly, attends church and loves singing hymns, and, even if she's not sure who it is she is praying to, she does believe her prayers are being heard. It is perhaps quite a remarkable and refreshing attitude to find in someone like her, when church is no longer considered hip or cool, that she is not shy or ashamed to say that she still attends. She started going several years after she got clean from the drugs and alcohol, because 'the vicar was so amazing and unjudgemental, and he's still one of my best friends'. Despite there having been some very tough times in her life, she admits, to this day she still believes that her faith, whatever it is, has helped her through most of them.

Perhaps one of those times was when she had a cancer scare a year after her marriage. 'The way I treat my breasts changed considerably after a routine check-up with my GP, which uncovered a lump. I had to have a biopsy but it turned out that I have big glands in my boobs. I'd never really considered breast cancer to be something I had to worry about, but, when I got the test results back and I knew it was all right, I burst into tears. I think I'd been trying to stay strong to prepare for a bad result.'

Sadly, her marriage to Leggett would not survive that long. Just three months after the whirlwind romance, they went their separate ways. Davina was quickly telling friends she wanted a divorce. Not that she had ever told anyone apart from her very closest pals. For some, it was Davina's best-kept secret. Their curious relationship is something Davina and her mother Florence have steadfastly refused to discuss ever since the split. It is also something that Leggett, interestingly enough, has been legally prevented from speaking about. Naturally enough, this has led to much speculation concerning what could be said about the 12 weeks their union lasted.

'I'm a mixture,' she says. 'I'm deeply insecure, but I have a huge ego.' She did, after all, go through years and years of counselling to come to terms with being abandoned by her mother, and so it is perhaps not surprising that she had issues with 'sharing', which she later admitted did wreck this, her 'first disastrous marriage', as she calls it. Apart from that, the very few times she has talked about the marriage, she gives no real clues as to why it may not have worked. Quite the opposite, in fact: 'I was madly in love,' she says. 'We rushed into our relationship. It didn't work out – it was wrong, so I got out quick and it's been a very painful experience. The major thing about making a marriage work with two people is that you respect the other person, their career and what they go through. That's all I really want to say about it. It's a very private matter for both of us.'

Not long after the split, and perhaps quite unexpectedly as far as Davina and Leggett were concerned, the tabloid press turned it into a public affair when they reported that the couple were back together, even though this was not the public perception of the relationship, or even that of Davina's neighbours.

Not surprisingly, many didn't even know what Leggett looked like as he had never been photographed by the paparazzi before. To make matters worse, according to neighbours, the so-called 'back together' was nothing of the sort. What happened, explained one onlooker, was when Leggett turned up at Davina's place for a chat. But it was not long before the apparent 'emotional heart to heart' spilled outside into Davina's communal front garden in a quiet London street and things got out of control.

It was when Davina and Leggett's voices could be heard screaming at each other that the neighbours realised something was not quite right and soon had their net curtains raised to discover there was one 'hell of a row' going on, right outside their windows for all to see. 'We could hear them halfway down the street. It was all very emotional and it looked like Davina was breaking down in tears. It was impossible to avoid eavesdropping since we didn't have ear-plugs. They seemed to be talking about their marriage and how to resolve matters. It looked like they were very keen on each other still, but couldn't sort out their differences. Andrew eventually had enough and went off home, but Davina ran after him. They seemed to end on better terms. We're all hoping they did – anything but another row like that one.'

Although to most who knew them their relationship

clearly was over, many were quick to notice Davina did not remain alone for long. By the February following her split from Leggett, one month after she had started filming the first series of *Streetmate* for Channel 4, she was spotted on the arm of Stan Collymore. She was still getting over the end of her marriage to Leggett when she apparently fell for the then 27-year-old striker.

Born in Staffordshire on 22 January 1971, Collymore was, without question, an accomplished centre forward, who, it is perhaps true to say, became equally famous for the controversy he caused off the field. Collymore was like most footballers who seem to come out of nowhere to achieve unprecedented greatness. He started out in the non-league game with Stafford Rangers before being given the chance of a lifetime as a full-time professional with Crystal Palace at the age of 19. Although he dropped down the divisions to Southend United, while there he scored such a huge amount of goals that he was given a second chance in top-flight football by Nottingham Forest, and, despite rumours of fallouts with team-mates, Collymore's goalscoring record with Forest was so phenomenal that Liverpool offered a club record bid of £8.5 million for him.

Scoring a spectacular goal on his Liverpool debut, he began a fruitful, enigmatic and controversial two-year spell with the club. His career highs included scoring frequently in a superb partnership with Robbie Fowler and winning two caps for England, but the low points were equally spectacular. In one year, he was fined after refusing to play for the reserves, refused to move closer to Merseyside from his home town of Cannock, publicly criticised manager Roy Evans and his tactics, and played badly in the 1996 FA Cup final against Manchester United during which he was substituted and Liverpool lost 1–0.

Collymore and colleagues Jamie Redknapp, David James and Steve McManaman were labelled the 'Spice Boys', a term used to signify the players who were playboys of the game, and it was probably true. Collymore infamously got into further spats with his colleagues over that very innuendo and publicly declared he was 'not a Spice Boy' and hated the fact that he should even be called one. Though undoubtedly one of the great footballers of his day, he set himself up for a head-on collision with his club that made a transfer inevitable and, compounded with the emergence of Michael Owen through Liverpool's ranks, the mixed-race striker was sold to Aston Villa in 1997 for just £1 million less than his record price tag two years earlier.

Becoming more eventful off the pitch than on, Collymore's time at Villa was probably his undoing, and one that seemed marred by his long-term treatment for depression which led to him being out of favour with manager John Gregory, successor to Brian Little, who had brought Collymore to the club in the first place. In the three years he spent at Villa, Collymore scored only 15 goals and got himself sent off several times, including once for shoving a young Michael Owen to the ground in a game against his old club in the same year he met Davina. One year later, his form had deteriorated so significantly that he was loaned out to Fulham for two months in the hope that it would reignite his career. It didn't.

To make matters worse, three months after he had met Davina at a Julian Clary concert, he called her up to tell her he was resuming his relationship with his ex-girlfriend Ulrika Jonsson, another popular television presenter. Today, Ulrika sums up her life as someone who's been married, divorced, faithful and unfaithful; battled with depression; enjoyed moments of bliss; had an abortion; been raped and stripteased; told black and white lies; has loved herself and loathed herself. She was, at one time, the woman most men fantasised about and would most like to have sex with. So it was no surprise that Davina was upset when Collymore decided to return to Jonsson not long after he had split from the former weathergirl.

Yes, sure, Davina confessed, 'I was upset. It was the

end of something. I had been in the doldrums after my marriage break-up, and Stan and I had a lot of fun together. We really enjoyed each other's company and it had been an uplift for me. Obviously, it was not my decision but you can't argue with someone who is being totally honest with you. I really respected him for telling me the truth and not letting me look like an idiot.' All the same, she continues, 'Stan told me the stuff with Ulrika was dead and buried. But now he's gone back to her. We're still friends, but a loss like that is the end of a dream – something that you think had potential and it doesn't any more.' It was partly for that reason that they would remain friends: 'If he had been cheating on me behind my back, I would not be speaking to him. I really can't fault him.'

Collymore had first spotted Jonsson in August 1997, a few days after her 30th birthday during a party that the crew of the *Gladiators* ITV game show had organised for her. She had presented the successful series for seven years of its eight-year run as the most popular programme on primetime Saturday-night television. The party was also attended by players from Aston Villa football club, or so rumour had it. It wasn't until Jonsson returned to her hotel after dancing the night away that she found out that, as word had it, some of Villa's players had, in fact, turned up. One in particular, who obviously had his eye on her, had already left his mobile-phone number for her to call the next day. Knowing very little about football and less about Collymore, she called up her brother and a colleague to find out more, and, following their positive responses to her questions, she was now curious to meet with the football player who was so interested in her. Armed with a copy of the *Daily Telegraph*'s sports pages and egged on by her sister and her friend, she decided after much self-debate that, yes, she would meet with him.

What had started out as perhaps an inquisitive lunch date, as far as Jonsson was concerned, soon turned into a fully fledged affair. One week after they met, the couple had their first dinner date at Quaglino's in London. The very next day – the same day that news had broken about the tragic death of Diana, Princess of Wales in a motoring accident in France – they got engaged. Soon after, they were living together in the new house that Jonsson had recently moved into just days before her new television show *It's Ulrika!* aired.

But, within a few weeks of their engagement, the relationship would run into trouble and suffer a number of problems that were to plague their time together.

Not even their separation, during which time Collymore dated Davina, seemed to improve matters. Although at first Collymore's reconciliation with

Jonsson may appear to have got off on a better footing, it would not last. In her autobiography, *Honest*, Jonsson, told how their second try at romance quickly deteriorated with Collymore continuing to shout abuse at her. Despite her concerns, she still went on holiday with him, an experience she called 'truly, the worst of my life'. It was shortly after that holiday that something happened that would end their relationship for good.

It was during the World Cup in France, in June 1998, that the unthinkable happened. Jonsson had chosen to stay in a Paris bar pulling pints for fans, with actor Ewan McGregor and fellow television host Ally McCoist and BBC Scotland staff rather than dine with Collymore alone. And that is when the trouble began. It seemed that 'Mr C', as Jonsson called him, was jealous that she was partying with Scots fans before the opening match against Brazil. But what happened next took Jonsson and others completely by surprise. 'As I walked through the doorway, I felt him grab me by my forearm and before I knew it I had crashed on to the floor,' Jonsson recalled in her book that was published four years later. 'The next thing I felt was his foot against the left side of my head, then the right side and then the left side again. I remember putting my arms up for protection and the force of his further two blows hitting my arms. A loud, high shriek came from my mouth – I didn't recognise it. It didn't sound like me, and with that I felt myself fall backwards down the stairs into the cellar. I carried on screaming, even though there were no more blows. I could barely look up, but saw two men restraining Stan. I carried on shrieking. I didn't know what happened.' Needless to say, the couple – who had been together overall for 18 months – split up the following day.

In the days that followed, after news of the horrendous attack on Jonsson broke in most of the national press, Collymore became a national hate figure when he admitted to punching her during the argument. And, if there was any doubt or disbelief that such a thing could happen, Jonsson was photographed with bruises from the attack on show. Collymore, on the other hand, suggested that the bruises on Jonsson's face were, in fact, a reflection of raindrops from the lens of the photographer's camera. In the years that followed, he would even take a swipe at Jonsson's telling of the story, saying he was 'disgusted at the inaccuracies and misportrayal of the relationship as a whole and the events prior to and during the now-infamous trip to Paris'.

Making matters worse, of course, was when the *News of the World* ran a story that another of Collymore's former fiancées claimed that she had been beaten half to death by him on several occasions.

Alongside the story ran a diary of his rather chequered inglorious past. Jonsson felt sick that 'he had done it before, this had been no accident: he wanted to hurt me'. And it didn't end there. Some years on, there seemed no let-up in the Collymore versus Jonsson tirade when Collymore lost a court order banning him from selling an explicit video of the pair indulging in sexual activity. He was told he could not sell video footage, stills or photographs showing Jonsson naked or having sex with him and must hand over all his material to her lawyers.

The video, said to have been made on holiday in Jamaica, showed explicit scenes of the two making love. A statement from Jonsson's lawyers said, 'We note from press reports that it is said that certain material – principally a video recording but possibly other material – has been offered to various newspapers with a view to publication concerning our client. The reports indicate that the material – which is obviously private and confidential in nature – was being offered by a representative of Mr Stan Collymore.' Jonsson's lawyer continued that his client 'is extremely relieved and pleased to note that the press have, commendably, declined to purchase or publish such material for which our client is very grateful'. The *News of the World* declined to buy the video after it was offered to them.

The video was offered two days after the first extract from Jonsson's serialised autobiography appeared.

Adding fuel to the fire was the three-day sanctuary and breather Davina provided Collymore at her villa in the South of France. If there were any concerns about why she should rush to his defence, the answer was very simple: 'I still adore him. He is sensitive, very gifted, funny, loyal to his mates and really down to earth. With me he has never been anything but a true gent.' And, although she would describe the attack on Jonsson as unforgivable, and agreed that Collymore did need help, she finally lost her patience and snapped, 'Just because he has done something silly doesn't mean I never want to talk to him again. I have done lots of silly things in the past and I will in the future. I hope that my friends wouldn't drop me [if I did something silly].'

And even though she was supporting him through the troubled aftermath of the saga, it did not mean for one minute that she was about to rekindle her relationship with him – far from it. Davina herself had been through troubled times herself. Talking on a rare occasion about her first marriage, Davina said, 'I was madly in love,' she repeated. 'It was very exciting and I got carried away. Sometimes things like that work and sometimes they don't. I'm still in touch with Andrew and I'm recovered now, but it was hard for both of us. I would love to marry again. I haven't given up hope. I am madly romantic and an idealist, and I'd like to have a family and meet someone I can relax with. If it happens, it happens.'

What's interesting about Davina, agree most who have interviewed her, when she talks about matters of the heart, is that 'she is outspoken without being offensive, clever without being smug, and she is a babe without being a Living Doll' – and certainly that was the case here. If you consider that she had been through her own treadmill, it shouldn't be that difficult to work out why she would want to do all she could to help Collymore. Whether it was Davina or Collymore's decision to make, it was clear that he needed some kind of guidance about counselling in a bid to control what he himself called his violent temper. 'I'm not justifying what he did, but change is possible for everyone. He has got to deal with his anger, just like I did with drinking,' she said. And certainly as far as Davina was concerned that's what he wanted help with. She was only too willing to guide wherever she could, with anything that might help him take the right steps to sort himself out – which according to Davina he was.

'He gets accused of not doing enough to get himself out of a vicious circle,' she continued. 'But people don't know what he is doing to help himself behind the scenes. I don't understand what happened between

Stan and Ulrika because I was not there and I'm not going to judge their relationship. Stan has got to sort himself out, but he is still a friend of mine and I believe he is a good man. It's a tragedy what's happened. I never saw that side of him. He was very gentle. I don't know if different women press different buttons with Stan. I would not dare go into it because, even if someone does press buttons, it doesn't justify violence. I have had arguments with people, exploded and done things I regretted and smashed plates.'

Smashed plates or not, four months after Collymore had attacked Jonsson in Paris, the first of the 10 episodes of Davina's new series *Streetmate* premièred on Channel 4 in the evening primetime viewing slot. With filming completed earlier in the year, Davina had already scoured the country to find perfect partners for some of those among Britain's millions of single people. After grabbing them off the street, viewers were treated to a fly-on-the-wall peek into how each contestant prepared for their date and, more importantly, how the actual date itself progressed and ended up. Interestingly enough, soon after it started its Wednesday-night run, *Streetmate* was already in the running to become the new 'real-life' alternative to challenge Cilla Black's *Blind Date*, which by then was in its 13th year and struggling with an audience of 5 million less than the 15 million it had started out with.

Perhaps much of the appeal for Davina and *Streetmate* was the fact that she simply loved matchmaking, doing her bit to help some folk find love. 'Nothing makes me happier than to introduce two people who hit it off. I'm a chronic matchmaker. All my friends groan when I say, "Hey, I've someone I want you to meet", because they know what they're about to get into.' Perhaps that's why, as Ian Hyland writing in the *Sunday Mirror* put it, 'She always seemed to be ambushing strangers in the style of a particularly disciplined spaniel. Not that her trademark eagerness has hindered her career; on the contrary, it defines her success.'

Streetmate was, continued Hyland, her first big break 'in which Davina would ambush strangers in the hope of them turning out to be suitable date material. She especially enjoyed hurdling street furniture as she closed in on her target. It made it all seem that much more of an adventure. Once she nabbed someone, she'd brandish her microphone and move on to her speciality – the breathless interview.' She was, most others agreed, by this time well on her way to becoming a serious contender in the celebrity stakes. And *Streetmate* certainly helped. But unlike the Poshes and Denises of this world, concluded Hyland's feature, 'She is not a slave to designer originals and round-the-clock grooming. She looks great in a pair of funky denims and a dab of lipgloss. Boys love her for her looks and girls love her for her wit and bubbly personality.'

But not everyone was as thrilled with the show. In one episode, filmed on the streets of Manchester, Lisa Jones and Jason Winstanley were introduced to each other. Despite finding romance on their first date and moving in together fairly quickly, three months on, things had altered. Lisa claimed it took 'half an hour' for the film crew to coax her into taking part. Four hours into the search Davina told her she had found her the perfect date, to which Lisa responded, 'I've been in Manchester for four years and haven't found one, so I don't think you'll have found it in four hours.' Love at first sight, it certainly wasn't, according to Lisa ('When she introduced me to Jason, I couldn't stick him. He was everything I can't stand in a bloke – gobby, cocksure and arrogant'). She remembers turning to one of Davina's crew and saying, 'He's a complete idiot!' However, later that evening as the date progressed (and after a few glasses of wine) she allowed her initial perception of Jason to change, 'I began to think there was a spark. I knew behind the laddish exterior there was something more.'

The couple met for a drink a few days after their first date, but they didn't sleep together for about three weeks, which led Lisa to believe that this was more than a casual relationship ('I really did think I was beginning to fall in love with him. He's a lot more sensitive than he seems. I had reservations about moving in with him because I'd only split up with my last boyfriend two days before I'd met Jason. But I thought, "Well, maybe it will work."') Lisa and Jason moved into a shared house, which meant they didn't get any privacy and after a few weeks they began to drift apart. Eventually there was one weekend when she didn't see Jason for three whole days; he didn't even phone. When he finally came home, she flew at him. Unfortunately it kept happening, with the inevitable outcome. Lisa said, 'After we split up I cried for hours with the relief of it all ending. I knew that I wouldn't have to deal with it any more. If it wasn't for *Streetmate*, Jason and I would never have got together. We had nothing in common. The other night I asked myself, "Do I still love this guy?" I definitely don't. But I love him as a mate.'

Jason's view of things is slightly different: 'Davina came into the shop and asked me if I'd go on a date. As soon as I saw it was Lisa, I said, "I'd love to." I'd split up from my girlfriend two months before and was on the lookout. I wasn't going short – I was beating off girls with a stick. From the moment Lisa got out of the taxi we didn't hit it off. I thought, "This is going to be a nightmare."'

He recalls that after a meal, the couple went on to a

hotel, where they shared a bottle of champagne. But, 'although we'd been together for hours, we still didn't know each other. But immediately the cameras stopped filming the barriers came down. We kissed… and we're talking tongues.'

At the time Jason was living in Wigan and Lisa lived in Manchester. Testing the water, he told Lisa it was too far (and too late) for him to get home. Lisa offered her sofa, and according to Jason, 'that is where I stayed. If she had slung me into bed that night, it would have been too easy. I wouldn't have had any respect for her.' The next day the two met up again in the evening for drinks and after a week, they began sleeping together. Things went from strength to strength ('She told me she was in love with me and I said I felt much the same. When a mate offered Lisa a room in his flat, I moved in, too. I didn't think it was a big step because I wanted to be back in Manchester. I had no expectations, but we thought we would just go for it. At the beginning it was excellent.')

However, as the relationship progressed, it faltered and Jason spent more and more time out drinking. Eventually Lisa sat him down and told him he was never there. In an effort to put things right, Jason said he would try and spend as much time as he could with her. But, as he says, 'I made the effort for a couple of days and then went back to my old ways. I am very selfish. But maybe I didn't feel like I loved her any more. We had stopped having sex. Lisa has told me that she's still in love with me, but I'm not at all in love with her any more. We have nothing in common, but I do care about the girl and I have respect for her. We will definitely stay firm friends.'

There was a feeling of love in the air during the production of *Streetmate* and it was something that would also affect Davina herself. 'I was in a restaurant and there was this gorgeous waiter, and I was thinking, "Where's my *Streetmate* person?"' At that time, she was beginning to write a new guide to snaring a man called *The Dating Game*, in which her author's note commented, 'I may be an odd candidate to write this book. I've had a string of interesting, exciting and sometimes disastrous relationships and one failed marriage. So what do I know? I know a lot!!!' Although the book was just her take on things, she did find 'the whole relationships thing gripping: why do some work when others don't, and how come some of the most successful, gorgeous charismatic women in the world can't find a man? And some of the most delicious men I know are stuck being single? Well, I've got some far-flung ideas on how to be a go-getter and all woman. And on the best way for all you delicious men to deal with us. I'm giving them a trial run myself and I'm having the time of my life.'

It was one of those fun paperbacks with an under-lying serious tone, and Davina's back-cover blurb automatically invites readers to take a closer look and at the same time perhaps tells us a great deal about who Davina is. 'I know what you want: you want hot dates, loads of sex and a morning after that turns into the rest of your life. So what's going wrong? I know that too, I used to be confused. I mean, what is all this? Girl Power, Ladettes, New Men, Alpha Males? It's a scary world out there and we need all the help we can get. Well, I've got it sussed now. And here it is for the benefit of Humanity and the Future of the Species. All you need to know to get out, get lucky and get loved up.' Her advice was simple. Gyms are good, blind dates are bad, and, as she would soon discover for herself, dog walking is excellent for developing relationships.

And she was right. But little did she know as she sat in that restaurant in the same year that *Streetmate* first hit the screens that she would soon be finding the true answer to love for herself and dedicating her book to the man who would eventually become her fiancé.

5

LOVE AT FIRST SIGHT

Towards the end of 1998 and one month after *Streetmate* had started its first series on Channel 4, Davina was recovering in a hotel room in Sydney, Australia after a stunt for her latest television project, *Don't Try This At Home*, had gone badly wrong. In fact, it had ended up just short of disaster. Screened in January of the following year, the series, in which members of the public participated in daredevil challenges, was another that quickly became the primetime Saturday-night show.

For Davina, the only downside was that, if any of the contestants lost their nerve to go through with the challenge they were prepared to try, then it would be up to her to step in and go through with the challenge herself. It was probably the excitement of watching a stunt that could possibly go wrong that turned *Don't Try This At Home* into such a hit show. Perhaps it is like that hidden or secret agenda said to exist in most of us, but none of us wants to admit to. When we watch motor racing, for instance, do we not become optimistic for an accident or, even better, a pile-up of cars to happen right in front of our eyes? As strange as it may seem to even think that such an unthinkable and fatal disaster could occur, it does appear to be something that we perhaps subconsciously hope for. As any psychotherapist would tell you, it is all to do with the adrenalin and excitement we feel we need to turn something as simple as motor racing into something much more exciting. Isn't that why Evel Knievel, like a Messiah, attracted so many followers to his stunt shows?

For the 'Challenge of a Lifetime' section of *Don't Try This Home*, it was the same: it was the highlight of the show. It was the moment when a viewer had written in for themselves or nominated another to try the impossible, their greatest personal challenge. This was done to either overcome a phobia, or just for a boast that they could do anything if presented with a dare. What happened was that Davina would turn up unannounced and ask the nominated to pick one of three envelopes, each with a different challenge inside given by a cryptic clue. They would then travel to the place of the challenge, which could have been round the other side of the world. The challenges would, however, ask more of an individual than they or anyone else could have imagined. They included some of the most unimaginable ideas one could think of – everything from hand-feeding sharks in Australia or jumping down a 100-metre gorge in New Zealand on a wire descender to abseiling the tallest building in the Southern Hemisphere or driving a car across a huge drop on nothing but two slack wires. On another occasion, Davina drove a mini-Moke across two steel girders, fixed between a pair of 300ft-high cliffs.

So is it any surprise that walking across a plank bridging the gap between two 10-storey buildings in Sydney would have been a complete turn-off, even to those with the most resilient sense of adventure? Not if you don't like heights! And that, apparently, was what happened on this particular stunt. Trouble was, Davina didn't like heights either. According to one observer, she teetered across the plank, terrified of the height and also the drop to the ground. Despite being attached to a safety wire, she lost her footing. With cameras rolling, the entire heart-stopping moment was captured on film as Davina quite dramatically and frighteningly fell until her descent was prevented by the safety wire. Even after the fall when she was swung this way and that way sideways, and ended up being thrown against the side of the building before she was hauled to safety, all of it was filmed.

According to entertainment columnist Matthew Wright, Davina told a pal and others that she had never been so scared in her life. 'As soon as she stepped on to the plank she was petrified and by the time she got to the middle she was visibly shaking. She said it all happened suddenly. One minute she was on her feet, the next she was flying through the air. For one horrible moment she actually thought she was a goner. She was so shaken when the crew got her down she barely noticed her injuries. But, thankfully, after a check-up, medics declared Davina was not seriously hurt. But filming of the series, that was scheduled to be screened two months later, was suspended for one week while Davina recovered.'

Perhaps it was one of the reasons why, when Davina came to host the show alongside Darren Day (and for the second series with Kate Thornton), she said, 'The sheer size of the audience that it attracted, and the fact that I wasn't that well known, absolutely petrified me'. Maybe, agreed Wright, but, in person, he wrote in his showbiz column that then appeared in the *Mirror*, Davina is every bit as engaging as watching her on screen. 'She's chatty, smart and honest, often painfully so. There is also a vulnerability she can never quite hide, but it is her genuine openness that has won her a place in the hearts of the public.' Wright was another journalist to note that 'to women, she represents a best mate and big sister rolled into one and, though she admits to being a flirt, she is still the type who can be trusted. Men love her because she's feisty and fun, equally at home down the pub, or with her feet up in front of a telly.'

Davina, on the other hand, insists, 'It's not an act, believe me. On telly, I'm me, but in a very excited state, like I would be at a party or talking to my best friend. It's like I get a caffeine rush and it's taken me a long time to calm down. When I'm in the studio, waiting to come on stage and they're about to go "Davina, Davina", I'm on the verge of hysteria, thinking, "How did I get here?"' But she had got there through sheer perseverance and perhaps by being extraordinarily selective in the choices she made about the shows she wanted to be involved with.

For *Don't Try This At Home*, though, it wouldn't be the only time that she would scare herself half to death on the show. Just over one year later, she was faced with an even worse challenge that not even she thought she could do. In fact, at the time, it was probably considered to be one of the most terrifying moments on television: the moment when Davina had to bungee jump 700 feet out of a helicopter over

Arizona's Grand Canyon. No question about it, 'the worst thing I have ever done in my whole life,' she recalls today. 'I cried every day for a week. I'd wake up in the mornings and go to sleep at night with nothing but that experience on my mind.'

Certainly, she wasn't expecting contestant Jason Hutchinson not to go through with it, even though such a jump had never been attempted before. 'It was quite possibly the most terrifying thing I have ever done and I would never do it again. I just had to go into auto-pilot. I was dangling over the Grand Canyon with my eyes shut. Occasionally, I would open them and think they haven't got me to land yet. Please hurry up! But,' she continued to explain in Jason's favour, 'once you bottle out of something like that, you know you'll never do it. So I was up in this helicopter, having watched this guy unable to do it, and I was frozen with fear. I kept chanting a mantra: "This will be fun, this will be fun", but it was like being possessed by a mixture of total terror but also a drive to do it. I was laughing and crying, and refusing to look out of the window. When we were in position, this guy just looked at me, unwrapped my safety belt and started counting me down with his fingers – five, four, three, two, one – and I jumped.

'Looking back, it's weird watching yourself in that kind of terror. The jump itself happened so fast, I was terrified yet focused. I kept thinking, "When is the rope going to get tight?" It all happened too fast and I kept my eyes closed until I was left dangling upside down for about 10 minutes. And every time I opened my eyes I'd see a mile's worth of fresh air between me and the ground. I started crying and shaking, saying, "Just get me down!" I was freaking out.

'The guys on the ground held on to me as they lowered me down – that's the most dangerous bit because if they lower you too fast you could bash your head really hard. One guy later said he put his hand out and I got him in a death grip and wouldn't let go. It was terrifying but exhilarating.'

The daredevil stunt had all started when careworker Jason's girlfriend, Rebecca Fricker, had written in to the show saying Jason, who had already done a crane bungee jump, had boasted there was no challenge too scary for him. But 'curiosity killed me when I looked out into that abyss and I thought, "No way!" I asked the stunt guy to push me, but he said he couldn't. My own body wouldn't allow me, I was glued to the spot. So we came down and poor Davina had to do it instead.'

By this time, of course, she had met Matthew Robertson, which was the reason she recommended dog walking as excellent for developing relationships. Likened to something out of one of her *Streetmate* shows, it happened while she was, in fact, walking her dog, a rottweiler-labrador cross, which she named Rosie, in a West London park. 'He was walking his dog and I was walking mine,' she smiles. 'In fact, I saw his dog first – she's a boxer called Chloe. She walked round the corner and I thought, "What a nice-looking dog." Then Matthew followed and I thought he was rather gorgeous, too. So I said hello and he said hello back. From then on, I walked my dog every day and hoped to see him. Slowly we got chatting. It got to the stage where I was getting really dressed up in case I saw him.'

She explains, 'I'd been walking Rosie at my local park for a couple of years and I'd got to know a lot of the people who walked their dogs there too; we'd all made friends. So when they saw me all done up in dresses, sexy clothes and make-up, they burst out laughing, saying, "Davina, you're so transparent, we know what you're doing!" And I'd try and act all innocent. I got a lot of ribbing when I went to the park in my horse-riding gear, a little riding crop and jodhpurs one day.

'Matthew was also wearing nice clothes in the hope that he'd bump into me. In fact, he'd asked some of the other dog walkers what time I walked Rosie so that he could "accidentally" bump into me. Before he met me, he walked Chloe at 9.30am; suddenly he was waking her up for 7.30am. His poor dog was permanently tired and dopey – she probably wondered what was going on.

'When we met we'd talk and talk, and really got to know each other slowly, which was lovely. He'd been living in America for five years so he didn't know who I was, which was brilliant. It wasn't until a few weeks later, when he started talking to his friends about me and told them my name and that I worked in TV, that they said I was quite well known. When he discovered I presented *Streetmate*, where I accost people in the street and try to set them up on dates, he thought I'd got hidden cameras and was setting him up, until I assured him I wasn't.'

Elsewhere, it had been reported that, when she first spotted the former model and soon-to-be presenter of Channel 4's *Pet Rescue*, who was two years younger than Davina, she walked past him. But, determined to act on the spark she felt, she went round the park again so they could bump into each other for a second time. But, in other variations of this, some say she simply doubled back and struck up a conversation. And in one of Davina's simpler explanations of what happened, 'we were thrown together. He said hello and then walked off, and I thought to myself, "Run the other way so you can see him again."'

Perhaps because she had been married so briefly and, as she has already said, it was disastrous or perhaps because she had to all intents and purposes been dumped by Stan Collymore when he went back to Ulrika Jonsson, Davina had been playing it safe by the time she met Robertson. She had remained single for six months and was carefully taking time out from relationships. In the past, 'I'd rushed into things and got burned. It's best to wait, go slowly. I'm enormously impatient; when I want something, I want it now. That's what I was like when I meet someone. It's hard for people like me to hold back. Before, I'd have forced the issue if I wanted something to happen with a bloke. I believe guys like being in control and chasing a girl. So I'd arrived at a point in my life where I was re-examining my past mistakes and looking at where I'd gone wrong. When I met Matthew, I wanted him to do all the chasing; I wanted to feel like a female. I took it slowly and it worked. Six weeks later, he asked me out.'

And two weeks after that, they shared their first kiss. Before she met Robertson, she confessed, 'I'd always gone for the naughty-but-nice types, the type you can't even trust with other women, which was wrong. Not only that, it was tiring. I couldn't do that again. Matthew is a good person. When people meet him, they rave on about how solid and kind he is. He's very good for me. I don't know about marriage, you should ask him about that, but I've never felt this way before.'

Eighteen months on from when they set eyes on each other, the couple and their two dogs were all living happily together in West London, where Davina was now spending her spare time flicking through bridal magazines. To any observer, onlooker, outsider, or even any of London's star-spotters, their romance almost seemed like it was straight out of a far-fetched Hollywood movie.

It seemed it was about to become even more romantic when Davina and Robertson took a flight to America the year after they met to spend Christmas with his family. That was when he popped the question and presented her with a dazzling engagement ring. One month later, Davina was said to still be on cloud nine and anyone who had interviewed her then couldn't help but notice how she was still fiddling with the large diamond and platinum ring as if she wanted to draw attention to it. But isn't that what happy fiancées deeply in love do?

The actual proposal, says Davina, was 'a really big surprise, as you can imagine. He didn't quite get down on bended knees but I think he was a bit merry. He had hit the beer to get a bit of Dutch courage. I said "yes" after I got over the shock. Until I saw the box, I was too frightened to believe he was asking me to marry him because I thought he might suddenly go, "Joke!"'

As for the ceremony, perhaps not giving it too much

thought through sheer excitement, Davina explained, 'It is not going to be a huge wedding. There will be about 80 people, close family and mates. It depends if we can get married in a church because I have been married before. If we can, I would love to. I have no idea where it will be. It is a bit of a nightmare because everyone wants to get married in 2000. At the moment I'm buying every brides magazine going.' And she was.

Certainly, Davina had no qualms about taking the plunge again, despite the failure of her first marriage. Sure, 'you definitely think harder about it,' she said, reflecting on her decision to marry for a second time. 'When I said yes, I knew what was involved and I knew I didn't want to go through another divorce. It felt much more momentous to take that on. I felt like I was very well informed about it all, and this time I knew what I was getting myself into. We have lived together for about a year. I feel very good about it.'

According to one journalist, however, and slightly contradicting Davina's telling, Robertson *did* manage to get down on one knee during the busy flight. And Davina agreed immediately after Robertson had whipped a dazzling diamond ring out of his pocket and slipped it on her finger. It was then, according to another passenger on the same flight to Washington DC, that Davina apparently leaped up, and began charging up and down the aircraft, waving her engagement finger around: 'She looked so incredibly happy, and was whooping with joy.'

As always, one of those ubiquitous showbiz 'friends' was on hand to say that Davina 'is very much in love with Matthew. He's a lovely guy and thinks the world of her. She wanted to see how things worked out before she made any announcement. But now Davina is sure things are going to be just fine. They are besotted, but have kept their relationship quiet to get to know each other and make sure it's the real thing.' And possibly it was kept under wraps for so long, away from the prying eyes of the tabloid press, because Davina and Robertson 'prefer to stay at home rather than doing the celebrity circuit'.

At the time, Davina said, 'I am probably more at peace with myself now than I've ever been.' But that peace was about to be interrupted with a new television project that would change the course of her career forever, and establish her as even more of a television favourite than she already was.

6

MRS ROBERTSON

One week before her wedding to Matthew Robertson in June 2000, Davina's mind was racing with all sorts of different thoughts when perhaps she should have been focused only on the events that were about to take place in seven days' time. But she could not help thinking about her past demons that now, at this crucial time in her life, had returned to haunt and torment her. In her bid to face up to whatever was bothering her, she called her mother Florence and announced that it was time for a meeting, and asked if she was coming.

Not that she was talking about the wedding, but, far more brutally perhaps, about Narcotics Anonymous, which Davina herself had been attending since beating a six-year addiction to heroin, cocaine and drink. And she knew she had the perfect ally in Florence. For years, Florence had fought her own battle with alcohol. It was, she admits, only Davina's love and concern which brought her back from the brink of death after years of drinking binges. Yet the two hadn't spoken for at least two years. In some ways perhaps Davina still blamed Florence for her own string of addictions. And perhaps now she wanted to finally lay them to rest.

Even if Davina's timing was radically off, with her wedding just a week away, there was never going to be the right moment for what she wanted to confront. Is there ever a good time for any of us to discuss, whether it be with family, a friend or work colleague, the more heartfelt matters we all have to confront at some time or another in our lives? There are times in everybody's life when, suddenly and inexplicably, things seem to go wrong, or get on top of us, and it is at those times that the only answer is to confront them head on.

And if that's what Davina was going through, whatever stress and concerns she was facing, then Florence was there to help her battle with her fears. 'When she asked about the meeting just before her wedding,' Florence explained, 'I said, yes, and that was it, and we went. Davina was in tears and I was in tears. It felt like drawing the line under our terrible experiences and it marked a new start for us both. We both need those meetings. If I don't go, I know one day I will take another drink, and it is the same for Davina.'

To examine the similarities of their lifestyles is truly amazing. After all, both are attractive, charismatic women with failed whirlwind marriages behind them and, on top of that, they have an almost parallel history of addiction. 'I was drinking 24 hours a day,' Florence reflected. 'And it was Davina who made me realise I was killing myself. She gave me the strength to know that, if she could give up drugs, I could stop drinking.' The turning point came in 1995 when Davina was visiting her mother, who by then was on her fourth marriage, to South African diplomat Henry Cock. 'I was drunk and aggressive, completely overboard as you are when you are drunk. She waited until she got home and then wrote to me and said, "Mum, I love you. I want my old mum back. I want you to get better." It was a simple heartfelt message.'

But for Davina it wasn't quite as simple as picking up a pen and putting down her thoughts on paper. To get to that moment, of actually writing the letter and mailing it, was a different matter entirely. Before she could do that, or felt that she could, she would attend five meetings of Alcoholics Anonymous. And, let's be truthful, to a recovering drug addict who used group therapy to kick the habit, the surroundings must have reminded her of experiences of which she perhaps didn't want to be reminded. But she knew only too well that her mother was drinking herself into an early grave and how else could she find the courage to tell her, to help her?

Not only that, but, as Florence now says, she imagines Davina would have been pretty well frightened about sending it. She probably thought 'that I would never talk to her again so she went to AA meetings to see what went on; she showed the letter to all these people, saying, you are an alcoholic – what do you think? The truth is, I owe my health and my sanity today to that letter. I would have been dead without it.'

Florence had started drinking when she was 28, and almost echoing Davina's words when she came off drugs: 'To start with it was fun, but it wasn't fun for long. Davina was the first person to say to me, "Look, you have a problem with alcohol. I think you should go to AA," and, yes, suddenly I realised I was making my own daughter suffer when I was drunk and I had to change. She knew that, if she could make it, so could I. From then on, I set out to try to change my ways.'

As was the case for Davina and her drug habit, it took courage on Florence's part to accept the inevitable. To start with, and like almost every other alcoholic or drug addict who has trouble recognising that they do indeed need professional help, Florence was already in denial. She denied she had a problem and, in her rage, she tore her daughter's letter to shreds, simply because her pride was unable to stomach the demand that she tackle her alcoholism. As far as she herself was concerned, she didn't have a problem: 'I thought, "How dare she? Who does she think she is?" I was sulking for weeks before I was able to phone her.'

Davina, of course, could read the telltale signs, having lost years and years from her addictions to heroin, cocaine and drink between the ages of 18 and 24. Although she had the help and support of such close folk as her half-sister Millie, and friends Sarah and Eric Clapton, the final push for her was after she learned the awful truth that one of her closest friends had died from an overdose. It was this that made her give up the addiction that might have killed her had she continued. Although Davina often and openly admits that she wasted six of her most precious years on drugs and alcohol, Florence blames herself for her daughter's descent into her addiction, accepting she was hardly a role model. 'I spent 30 years of my life boozing,' she says. 'Addiction is a genetic disease and I felt very guilty because Davina also got that side of me. In fact, even though we do not look alike, we are very similar in character. Her dad Andrew often says, "Oh, you are just like your mum."

'In fact, Davina suffered a lot by my breakdown

with Andrew. I was staying with friends and couldn't have her with me. It wasn't easy and I regret that she suffered, but I thought the arrangement was the best thing for her.' She believes a lot of Davina's problems began when she was sent to live with Andrew and his new wife Gaby: 'She had been brought up a country girl, all horses and piano lessons, but then she found herself in the big city. It made her insecure, unsure of herself. Even now she is still really a fragile person.'

It was only in 1996, four years after Davina gave up drugs, that Florence found out about her daughter's past. The revelation came in an emotional meeting in London following the letter Davina had sent six months previously. It was 'because of my problems,' Florence says, that, 'I never noticed what was happening with Davina. There is a lot I still don't know about it, things she wants to protect me from as her mother. Now she is very motherly towards me.' Not surprising really when you consider that Davina was very hurt by her mother and angry with her for longer than she herself realised, but like all of us, whether we have divorced parents or not, we need our mums – only in Davina's case, she wasn't there for her.

Today, Davina is less tempted to place all the blame at her mother's doorstep: 'Since I've come to terms with my own problems, I've been able to get much closer to her. It made me realise that, just because she had made a mistake in her life, it didn't automatically mean that she was a bad person.' Hence, the importance she felt of the pre-wedding trip to Narcotics Anonymous. Florence agrees: 'There was nothing better than that meeting; it was something that touched me so much that I can't explain it. It was also the first time we had seen each other in two years. We don't see each other enough. Things were different in my day. My father was a doctor, my mother a Catholic Spanish woman, and, even if you drank too much, no one talked about it. I was brought up assuming AA was for old tramps, not for people like me.' She jokes in a way at the irony of it all, when she told Davina, 'Maybe I should have put you down for AA or NA when you were at school while other people were putting their children down for Oxford.'

As for Davina marrying Robertson, Florence couldn't be more pleased, and, although she was retaining her silence about Davina's first and short-lived marriage to Andrew Leggett, she had no such problem about Robertson. 'Being a mother, you want to be sure your daughter is marrying the right person and Matthew is a terrific guy. He really understands her; he knows how she works.'

Florence has been completely taken aback by Davina's huge success on television but perhaps she was not entirely surprised by her daughter's choice of career. 'Even when she was very young, you could see she was very much a performer. My father always said she would become a comedienne or an actress because she had such a talent for putting on shows. I just think of her as my "Nanou", that's my nickname for her.'

Ironically, Florence has never seen any of *Big Brother*. Nor, from her home in South Africa, has she seen more than the occasional video of previous successes such as *Streetmate* and *Don't Try This At Home*. Pleased as she is by her daughter's career, it is Davina's success against drugs that Florence sees as the real achievement: 'I am extremely proud of her in that sense, as I know what it takes to stop because I have been there. I am incredibly proud, too, that she wasn't ashamed to come out and admit her problem. Davina and I had the same problems, and I am sober now because of her. She realised that she was out of control and had to do something to stop it. There is nothing to be ashamed about. And that applies to Davina, too.'

With offers of small-screen work for Davina then coming in by the sackload, much the same as it is today, Davina's drugs nightmare behind her and the joy of her marriage to Robertson, no one could be happier than Florence: 'Other people become famous and get into drugs. She did it the other way round. But today she just does her job and comes home every day a very normal person. Her popularity hasn't changed her. And she still goes to meetings of Narcotics Anonymous once a month. It would be easy for her to say, "I'm Davina Robertson now, I'm famous and I don't need to go." But she doesn't.' As for Florence, she had her last drink on 7 January 1998, a landmark known in AA circles as her birthday. She says that, exactly one year later, 'Davina called me and said, "Happy Birthday, Mummy." It meant so much to me.'

For the wedding itself, Davina had decided right from the word go that it wouldn't be featured in any glossy celebrity weeklies, such as *OK!* or *Hello*. As far as she was concerned, it was a private affair and that is how she wanted to keep it. Not that it would prevent the usual turnout of photographers, all fighting for that exclusive picture that they didn't really succeed in snapping. She had also decided to opt for a traditional wedding ceremony, something else she had always wanted. Despite the wedding being in the Millennium year, when everyone was deciding to get hitched, Davina and Robertson managed to find exactly the right location to seal what many had called a *101 Dalmations* romance in the village of Eastnor, near Ledbury, Hereford and Worcester.

According to some quarters of the tabloid press lucky enough to witness some of the day's events,

Davina arrived fashionably late at 3.30pm at the picturesque 19th-century St John Baptist Church for a 45-minute service. Carrying a small bouquet of cream and pink roses, and wearing a £10,000 white strapless floor-length dress by designer Vera Wang and decked out in Jimmy Choo shoes, she smiled and waved at gathered photographers and about 50 fans, who lined the streets and churchyard. She was accompanied by her bridesmaids: Jane Wood, who was wearing a strappy pink floor-length dress, and Claire van Gogh, sporting the same dress in lilac.

Matthew arrived 45 minutes earlier, wearing a charcoal Hackett morning suit with pinstripe trousers, a pale-yellow waistcoat and a silver cravat. After talking with family and friends, he went into the church with best man Sam Gardham just 15 minutes before Davina arrived. Afterwards, Davina, who had done what most brides do and kept her man waiting, refused to let a downpour of rain spoil her day – in fact, quite the opposite. She told waiting fans that so far, 'It's been a marvellous day, absolutely wonderful. It's been fantastic.' But then again, what wedding day isn't?

For the 'lavish' reception at Eastnor Castle, which the couple had hired out for £5,000, they insisted on keeping the whole affair more intimate than most celebrities do, with a moderate 80-name guest list. This was mostly made up of friends and family, as well as some of Davina's closest showbiz pals, such as Gaby Roslin and Julian Clary. Davina was given away by her father Andrew – the other 'love of her life'. In some ways, the talk of the day, as far as some journalists were concerned, was her mother, Florence, who had flown in from South Africa. That was probably something to do with Florence's agreement to speak out for the first time to the press about her daughter: her success, past demons and how they had now made up after a two-year hiatus; how they had, as far as they were concerned, locked away their skeletons into a Pandora's box that was not to be reopened.

Of course, as Davina noted, 'Showbusiness marriages are notoriously precarious, but I think we cope because we are a really normal couple at home. When two people work like we do, you have to respect what the other does, their career and aspirations. I don't think it is important that I married someone who can understand me. I think it is important I have married someone who I understand: his emotions, his feelings. The danger of our jobs is that you can become self-important and think the world revolves around you. I love Matthew to such a degree that he is the most important person in our relationship as far as I'm concerned.'

Perhaps what is even more interesting is that, as Davina says, 'I have never had any big plan for my career whereas I have with my personal life. I've always had this plan that I would get married, live in the country, have ponies, Vietnamese pot-bellied pigs and children tugging on my dress while I'm cooking a fantastic fish pie.'

Although having children was something she still had to do and the couple were living in Davina's West London home, it wouldn't be long before home met with the criteria she had so long desired: a £700,000 home in what is described as the millionaires' village of Woldingham in Surrey. It would be, according to journalists, a six-bedroom country pile with an acre of land and an indoor swimming pool. In the years to come, the couple would also put their minds to finding a ski chalet in Chamonix and househunting in St Tropez. Not that they would ever share the inside of their homes with the world through lavish spreads in *OK!* and *Hello*. While other celebrities may do this, as far as Davina and Matthew were concerned, like their wedding, this was a private affair. And can you blame them? For the time being, the important thing was that the house in Surrey that they found was just what Davina had dreamed of, and what could be better than that?

7

A BIGGER PICTURE

One month after Davina married Matthew Robertson, she took the biggest gamble of her career by agreeing to host what many were calling a TV bombshell – or, at least, that's what was hoped for. As one journalist asked, 'Remember Jim Carrey's film *The Truman Show*, about a man who realises his entire life is being recorded and that it amounts to nothing more than television soap opera? Well, Channel 4's *Big Brother* is the real thing.'

About to be launched on Channel 4, the show had taken its title from George Orwell's novel *1984*. *Big Brother* had already caused a political uproar in Germany and sparked heated public debates in Holland where, interestingly enough, the idea had been originally conceived. But when it was announced that it was now set for British television under the genial guidance of John de Mol, the executive of the now global production company Endemol, there were likely to have been some red faces among those who control what is suitable for British broadcasting.

Whatever fireworks were about to go off, Davina was looking forward to the reaction the first episode would bring. If nothing else, it was, as she pointed out, certainly going to keep her on her toes. 'It's unlike any other show I've done before,' she enthused. 'We've no idea what's going to happen so I have to be prepared for anything. I can't wait.' But, she admits, it is pretty much like 'a lottery whether you take a show on or not, but you have to ask yourself, "Would I be interested in seeing the show?" I saw a copy of the show from Holland and I loved it – fascinating viewing.'

The concept was simple. A selection of contestants, usually with an even split of male/female and with a diverse mix of ethnicity and sexuality, are picked randomly by the production company from auditions up and down the country and enters a specially built house. Twenty-eight cameras and 60 microphones monitor their every movement 24/7. The *Big Brother* house is also where each of the contestants, or 'housemates' as they would become known, would be isolated from the outside world, with no television, radio, telephone or internet connection. They would be completely cut off from their family and friends, and pretty much everything else. The only item the contestants could bring into the house with them was one suitcase of personal belongings and even then there was a limit on the number of items that each could pack. If lipstick, for instance, was brought in, then it could only be one lipstick per person. The same applied to such items as playing cards – just one pack only.

The aim, said Channel 4 at the time, was to offer viewers 'a laugh' or, as Davina puts it more precisely, to offer audiences 'a great opportunity to people-watch really closely and track relationships, bad and good. And the environment couldn't be more intense. I went to the programme launch in Cologne to spy out the land and what I saw convinced me that the box in the corner is now playing God.' As for the contestants taking part, this was certainly true, despite the lure of a £70,000 cash prize for the winner and the inevitable accompanying celebrity status.

Christophe von Borries, who devised the web of cameras the programme was relying on, also relied on the fact that 'other programmes have filmed people getting on with their lives, but always in the real world. They allow them to escape the cameras. But with *Big Brother*, once they are inside the house, everything they do is public. It's a bit like being laboratory mice, except mice don't have any choice about the experiments.' Adding to the fun (or the misery), and the only link to anything each of the 10 housemates would remotely have with the outside world, would be the *Big Brother* disembodied voice. The voice would set them bizarre tasks to perform at will and form the daily confessions of the Diary Room for all those outside of the house to see.

The twist was that every couple of weeks the contestants would have to nominate two of their housemates to go forward to a viewers' ballot which would then decide who gets thrown out of the house. The last housemate left wins the cash prize and their celebrity status, although in most cases, in this day and age of talentless instant fame, it was thought to be only short-lived. In her role as presenter, Davina would host the show live every Friday night during the run of the series from the *Big Brother* compound directly outside the house. She would reveal the latest person to be evicted from the house, based on who had received the most votes for eviction from the public, and would be there to prepare them for a potential hostile reception from the crowds and waiting press. She would then interview the evicted housemate about their stay inside the house as part of the live programme before showing them a compilation of their best bits of filming.

There were also some rules for Davina and the entire production team. As Davina explains, no one is allowed to talk to the housemates while the series is on: 'Nobody talks to them, not the producers, not anybody. Nobody can go in and say, "Hey, guys, could you just jolly it up a bit?" You'd love to sometimes but you can't because that would change the dynamics.' Nor did she want to know about any of the planned surprises simply because she can't keep secrets. If she did know, she says, she would be telling the whole world 'all the goss, and I'm not allowed to do that. I'm not great at keeping secrets; that's the bottom line. They'll tell me about the house and tasks, but they won't tell me about the housemates until about three days before.'

As Davina would probably agree, after watching a copy of the Holland show, the original series in the Netherlands had all the right criteria to make it into the national obsession it indeed became. When it first hit Dutch small screens in the autumn of the previous year, it was very quick to achieve ratings figures usually reserved for major cup finals and state funerals. So, if it worked there, why couldn't it do the same elsewhere? If there was any doubt about its success, one only had to be reminded that in Holland one *Big Brother* episode alone grabbed over 70 per cent of the viewing audience and millions logged on to the round-the-clock website.

In fact, for the Holland version of the show, the peak most probably came when Bart, a 23-year-old former soldier, successfully bedded Sabine, a pretty 24-year-old fashion stylist. Although it wasn't the most graphic sex scene in TV history, it didn't take much working out to see what was going on underneath the duvet. Now it was real people sharing a truly intimate moment and not just actors going through the motions. Filmed three years before Jordan and Peter Andre were seen fondling each other on camera in *I'm A Celebrity, Get Me Out Of Here!*, Bart and Sabine became famous for making out in front of the cameras that now focused on their every move, in and out of bed. And, if it happened in Holland, then why couldn't it happen in the UK as well? In fact, it was probably what the producers were banking on. If it's true that sex sells, then Channel 4 must have been hoping they could prove it.

What is interesting, perhaps, about the show in Holland is how an entire country was entranced by the idea of watching others having sex, and how both Bart and Sabine became celebrities in their own right because of it. Perhaps, too, other television networks could see the potential of similar 'will they do it or not?' situations. By doing so, asked some critics, was it inviting everyone to explore their own voyeuristic fetishes, and, if so, is that why *Big Brother* had become so popular on the Continent and had been sold around the world, making a fortune for its Dutch inventors in the process? And now that it was about to hit Britain, others asked, 'Has TV gone too far, has it got too big for its boots when it starts controlling people's lives of how they sleep, eat and socialise?' Not that any critical objections voiced anywhere would be enough to put off what seemed like 'the entire world and his wife' tuning into *Big Brother*. In fact, the show was so successful it took the nation by storm and soon made history by becoming one of the most popular shows ever to be broadcast on Channel 4; it also set new records for viewers' phone voting.

It probably helped matters when midway through the series the show hit the headlines when housemate Nick Bateman was ejected by the house for attempting to influence voting. Nicknamed 'Nasty' Nick by the tabloids, Bateman was confronted by his fellow housemates. The meeting, chaired by housemate Craig Phillips, remains one of reality TV's most memorable moments of the past decade. Nick denied the allegations presented to him that he had secretly written the names of other housemates on pieces of paper and shown them to other contestants in an effort to persuade them to nominate his choices. In the world of *Big Brother*, that was unforgivable and went against the rulebook that the housemates were expected to adhere to. And, after Nick's eviction from the house, with millions of viewers now hooked on the show, female housemate Melanie Hill was targeted for her flirtatious relationships with two other housemates, Andy Davidson and Thomas McDermott. It certainly made for compulsive viewing and, by the time the series came to a close, it was certain that it wouldn't be long before *Big Brother* would return for a second run. And what could be better than to have a *Celebrity Big Brother* as well.

Not that Davina was in any hurry to forget some of her own favourite moments from the first series: 'One of the big memories was when they first went into the house and got naked, and did imprints of themselves on the wall. The rumour went round that Craig was hung like a donkey. I thought that was quite funny and it was then that I realised this could be a really big programme because they'd all gone bonkers. It was very exciting. Then obviously the Nick moment was really, really good. There was another one-on-one moment from the first series that got me. It was when Anna was lying in bed and she was crying – she was just really weak and wanted to get out. And she was very quietly crying into her pillow, and then she sat up, she got her photos and she held them right to her face so that the cameras couldn't see what she was looking at, and she was looking at her girlfriend. Her

Davina started dating family friend Eric Clapton when she was 18 and he was 41. Their relationship lasted nine months. The pair are pictured here leaving the Ivor Novello Awards 1992 at The Grosvenor House Hotel in London.

Top left: A publicity shot from 1994, when MTV presented their new 'video jockies'.

Top right: Davina posing in 1997.

Bottom left: Davina and Tamara Beckwith pose in customised Wonderbras in aid of the Breakthrough Breast Cancer charity to support England and Scotland in the World Cup of 1998, the celebrations of which would bring a violent end to Ulrika Jonsson's relationship with Stan Collymore.

Bottom right: An early publicity studio shot from 1999.

Another rare studio pose from 1999 with Davina, revealing more cleavage than usual, in a black corset.

The Wild Ones! Davina and co-presenter Kate Thornton dressed up in motorcycle leathers to promote the second series of *Don't Try This At Home* for ITV in 1999.

Settling down. Davina and Matthew Robertson married in Eastnor, Herefordshire in June 2000. The couple had met two years before while walking their dogs in a West London park near Davina's home.

Davina is not only a favourite on the small screen but also loved by the tabloids.

Davina pictured launching her *30 Minute Workouts* fitness DVD at Woolworths in Milton Keynes just ten days before Christmas 2005.

Top: A photocall to announce the judges of *Pop Stars: The Rivals* was held in July 2002. Davina is pictured with Pete Waterman, Geri Halliwell and Louis Walsh.

Bottom: Working for charity. Davina at the Red Nose Day launch, in February 2005. She is pictured with (*left to right*) Elle MacPherson, Matt Lucas, June Sarpong, Dawn French and Konnie Huq.

girlfriend hadn't come out so she couldn't show anybody and yet Tania was going to come out on the show. It was just amazing, so sweet.'

But her all-time favourite moment wasn't even on camera: 'I was rehearsing a piece in the Diary Room. I'd left the house, and the director said into my earpiece, "Er, Davina, have you got your phone with you?" And I'd left it in the Diary Room! The housemates had got hold of it – thank God it wasn't switched on – and they were all looking at it in awe, going, "It's a phone!" They were all terrified by the sudden arrival of this piece of equipment. "What do we do with it?" "Shall we take it?" "Nooo!" It was just a phone! Anyway, *Big Brother* asked them to return it.

'Another favourite moment was when Craig gave his winner's money to his friend Joanne to pay for an operation, [that] literally brings me out in goosebumps. I also loved it every time Nadia got angry. I know that's an awful thing to say, but she was so fiery and passionate, and Mediterranean, and I love that. I love somebody who just says, "I am who I am, take it or leave it. I don't mind if you see me angry or if you see me crying."'

What is perhaps unbelievable about the heart and lung transplant Craig's friend Joanne Harris, who has Down's syndrome, needed was that the British medical system refuses to provide heart and lung transplants to people with this condition, despite the fact that heart disease is an inherent part of Down's syndrome. The only way for her to have the operation was to pay for it privately abroad, which had been a financial impossibility before Craig won the show. As Davina said, it was a truly touching moment that would bring a lump to anyone's throat who was watching.

Even so, according to online reviewer Ian Jones, neither the show nor Davina was flawless. He wrote, 'The actual first eviction was fumbled by Channel 4. Instead of waiting to reveal the result to both the viewers and the contestants at the same time, host Davina McCall told us first, thereby completely ruining the tension.' Unfortunately, five minutes or so before the phone lines closed Davina somehow managed to reveal the vote as it stood. As Ian Jones said, 'as if those remaining few minutes could overturn the outcome of the tens of thousands of calls already logged.'

For once, Davina seemed thrown and came under criticism for her handling of the whole affair. She was unable to recall Darren's name, frantically referring to him as 'the guy who's scared of chickens' and was completely off-balance on witnessing the other contestants' response to learning that Sada was the one chosen to leave (they all began cheering). Sada, meanwhile, cooed unconvincingly 'I'm so happy, I'm so happy.'

Events were divided between two separate live broadcasts, one at 8.30pm announcing the result, the other at 11pm when Sada left the *Big Brother* House. Some viewers felt that the atmosphere and build-up were completely flattened by this decision and would have preferred to stay with the events in the house all the way through, watching contestants come to terms with the result, seeing clips from the previous day, and so on.

As Sada left the house through the rain cries of 'Witch!' were heard. The post-eviction interview was a non-event. Davina and Sada were upstaged by screens on the wall behind them showing the housemates' wild celebrations following the result, which meant, of course, that everyone preferred to know more about what was going on inside the house rather than to listen to Sada for a second longer. Once more, Davina was exposed for not being properly briefed on the housemates' habits, though at no time had it been revealed that there were, in fact, two bi-sexuals in the house, not one. As online reviewer Ian Jones said, 'If C4, as *Big Brother*, supposedly sees and hears everything that goes on in the house, why weren't they prepared for this revelation from Sada in that post-eviction interview?' Finally, Davina made her ultimate gaff, running outside into the pouring rain to ask one of the crowd who would be thrown out next, only to receive the response, 'I want Nick out, he's such a prick."

The first *Celebrity Big Brother* was aired in March of the following year. Just a few months before the launch of *Big Brother 2*, it was produced in aid of *Comic Relief* as part of a joint effort between Channel 4 and the BBC. Lasting only eight days, a celebrity was evicted almost every night before viewers determined the winner. Proceeds from calls were given to *Comic Relief*, which celebrities Chris Eubank, Keith Duffy, Anthea Turner, Vanessa Feltz, Claire Sweeney, Jack Dee and, of course, Davina, hosting the evictions, all came out to support.

Ever since she presented the first series, and in the years to come with all the ones that followed, Davina's name would become synonymous with the show and her celebrity status rocketed her even further up the television ladder. Although she today acknowledges that she has much to thank *Big Brother* for, that's not the reason why her affection for the show remains so strong. For her, it is a deeper, purer relationship than one of expedience. This, she would tell you, is true love.

Indeed, even if she wasn't presenting *Big Brother*, or its *Celebrity Big Brother* spin-off, as far as she was concerned she would be one of those enthusiastic, faintly unsettling types in the crowd on eviction night, waving a homemade banner and screaming excitedly.

One can almost imagine it. The fact that she gets paid to turn up, meet the housemates and ask them questions is, to her, almost too good to be true. Certainly, it would be true to say today that, just as Davina needs *Big Brother*, the show depends on her fanlike enthusiasm, her chemistry with the housemates and her all-round jolly-hockey-sticks bonhomie.

And, from that point of view, there would be no reason on earth to think that she wouldn't have been as excited as the rest of the fans to see Jack Dee win the first of the celebrity editions and Claire Sweeney to follow in second place. The highlight, though, for everyone, and probably Davina too, had to be Jack Dee's escape from the house partway through the show when he got past the *Big Brother* security staff before returning after an hour. He told the other housemates he managed to get to Stratford before deciding to turn back. With or without the Jack Dee escape and Davina doing her usual, the show still managed to hit the headlines – this time over what appeared to be Vanessa Feltz going through a mental breakdown, which led to her scrawling various words relating to 'constantly being watched' in chalk on the kitchen table. But wasn't that the whole point of the show, to be constantly watched? One cannot help wondering why Feltz agreed to go into the celebrity house if she didn't like being watched.

Although critics expected the second series in May 2001 would be nothing more than a ratings flop, and prove that the success of the first series had just been a fluke, they couldn't have been more wrong. If anything, *Big Brother 2* proved to be the better of the two series. It had the best viewing figures, the best public voting for the eviction nights and the best moments from inside the house with world record attempts for the tallest sugar cube tower and, even more bizarrely, the most sweetcorn eaten within a limited time.

After the huge success of the first series, and with a much larger budget for the second, the house (which was located in Bow, East London) was renovated for the new batch of housemates. In an extra twist to the show, an eleventh housemate, Josh Rafter, entered the house a week later as the result of a public vote. It was a toss-up between him and two others. As was more or less expected, the series introduced another romance. This time it was the turn of Paul Clarke and Helen Adams to get up close and personal during the time they spent in the house.

Sure, their relationship probably helped in the ratings war as the series rolled on. But more so by the tabloids picking up on the speculation of the chances of the couple following in the steps of their international counterparts by having sex live on television, especially since Helen was already in a relationship on entering the house. Not that it would be the first or only time that a contestant found new love. Interestingly enough, and perhaps against all odds, they remained together after the show had finished and announced plans to marry, which, with Davina being the matchmaker she confesses to be, would have probably pleased her no end.

Not that she's interested in watching others having sex or even kissing; she's just intrigued in watching the slow unfold of two people realising they like each other. 'I love watching people relating to each other.' That's why the opening show is her favourite. 'Just watching people walk in, clock each other for the first time and thinking, "Oh, do they like each other?" or "Oh, she definitely doesn't like him," and then they end up falling in love.'

One of Davina's favourite experiences on the show was, in fact, Paul and Helen, 'because nobody saw that coming. Everybody kept saying Paul was playing her and I kept saying he wasn't, he really likes her, and it was almost in spite of himself. Because she was slightly ridiculed by the house, it wasn't cool for him to like her but there were bits of Helen he really adored. I could see that and I was so excited. And I was right: they're still together. I was just beside myself watching them fall in love – it was like the best soap opera I've seen in my life.'

But it wasn't just Paul and Helen's romance that was

winning over viewers, or Davina, for that matter. Irish housemate Brian Dowling became an instant hit with viewers and, after winning the series, would go on to launch a highly successful television career for himself. His success in and out of the house led to him being voted the most popular *Big Brother* contestant, up to and including the next three series that followed, which considering series seven was scheduled to start in May 2006 wasn't at all bad for anyone playing the popularity stakes.

By now, of course, it looked as if *Big Brother* was here to stay, and, despite the odd little critical objection, who better than Davina to be its host for as long as it lasted? Besides, 'I would be so angry if someone else was presenting *Big Brother* because it's mine and no one else is allowed it! I love that programme.' Whenever it's on, and on the nights she's not presenting, she is as hooked as anyone else, as apparently is husband Matthew. 'Oh, darling,' she tells him, as each series approaches, 'it's nearly coming to that time when we can snuggle up at 10pm every night and watch *Big Brother* together and then go to sleep discussing it. And he's like, "I know! I'm really looking forward to this series because, even when I don't think it's that good, it's still bloody brilliant!"'

8

MERELY AN ACTRESS

Television presenter wasn't the only role Davina was playing in May 2001; she had also made her first appearance as an actress. Even so, the role still wasn't as important as the one she would take on that September. Davina had already broken the news that she was expecting her first child. In fact, she announced it just five weeks into her pregnancy, presumably because of her busy high-profile schedule.

It wasn't long after that announcement that she and Matthew nearly came to blows during her scan when it came to discovering their unborn child's gender. 'I would love to know what sex it is, but Matthew won't let me,' she confessed. 'We had a domestic about it in the scanning room. I was going, "Please can I?" and he was going, "No." The doctor was saying, "I know what it is, do you want to know?" and I went, "YES!" and Matthew went, "NO!"'

Although she was looking forward to her first family Christmas – 'having a baby is a big thing and I'll probably take four months off after the birth' – and another series of *Big Brother*, right now she was putting her mind to the role that would mark her acting debut. It was to be on the small screen in a new, but all too short-lived, ITV sitcom. According to Mark Lewisohn's *Radio Times Guide to Television Comedy*, *Sam's Game* 'was another stroll through *Babes In The Wood* territory, with TV presenter/host Davina McCall flexing her acting muscle'. And indeed, though outshone by Ed Byrne as the hapless Alex, her performance was competent. Although the sum of *Sam's Game* was modest, there were good moments and, refreshingly, it 'steered clear of the tedious vulgarity that tainted contemporary flat-share sitcoms'.

According to an official synopsis, it was the story of four friends, who get involved in each other's lives and loves while renting flats in a large London house. Sam is big-hearted and gutsy, and is always up for anything, but underneath the confident image she is just as insecure as anyone else; Alex is her neurotic flatmate. But, just like most people having one of those days, she appears to be having one of those lives! Phil is Sam's neighbour, who is living proof of the maxim that those who live by the flirt die by the flirt – a man very much attached to his self-image of easy-going charmer. And Marcia is Sam's upstairs neighbour. She is also the waitress at their local café – a chronic gossip with big attitude. Sam and Phil are flirting friends, Sam and Alex are firm friends, and Alex and Phil are just friends through association with Sam, and Marcia thinks they are all good for a gossip.

Lewisohn, however, summed it up far more simply and precisely in his guide to comedy. It was, he wrote, about 'single girl Sam who lives in a pleasant flat, in a small apartment complex above a High Street shop. To help pay the inflated rent she illegally sublets to Alex, a pleasant but incident-prone Irishman. Across the hallway resides the hunky Phil. There is a spark between Sam and Phil but it has yet to ignite. Also on the scene is Marcia, who spends as much time in Sam's flat as in her own. The trials and romances of the quartet are the essence of the show.'

But not everyone would agree with Lewisohn. In his online review of the first episode, entitled 'Bed', Steve Bennett wasn't yet completely convinced. It had some good points but still lacked that something to turn it into an instant hit. And with a second series scrubbed, he was most probably right. Not only that but Davina's first foray into the sitcom world, he wrote, got off to a fairly shaky start, with a rather obvious half-hour of farce. 'Lacking any of the finesse of, say, *Frasier*, which manages to bring new subtleties to the genre, the opening episode of *Sam's Game* involved a clunking, old-fashioned tale of misunderstood actions and one-dimensional characters. Plot points were laboured so even the densest of viewers would know what was going on. "Hello, Sarah," said Ed Byrne's Alex as he picked up the phone. "My girlfriend," he explained to his flatmate of several months, who of course wouldn't know that.

'"The landlord's trying to find a loophole in the lease so he can evict me and sell this flat," the lovely Davina summarised at one point. This was like having a narrator, or watching comedy with subtitles for the hard of thinking. Thinly drawn characters – such as the tyrannical landlord or the battleaxe girlfriend whose only reason for existing was to issue threats to Alex, if he lied, did little to endear, too. But having said that, the writers' contrivances did conspire to a genuinely funny line on more than one occasion – and there can be no denying that McCall and Byrne exude a likeable charm on the small screen, despite their inexperience in the acting department.

'Tellingly, the best bits came away from the "Oops,

neighbour, there go my trousers" territory – Byrne's strangled attempt at an Australian accent was a pretty effective piece of comedy. If the series moves away from its broad farce to concentrate more on its central characters, there could yet be hope this develops into something a lot more interesting.'

Not that such comments would be of any surprise to Davina. If anything, she was surprised to be offered the part in the first place – especially alongside the likes of Byrne, even though he was a stand-up comedian, Tristan Gemmill and Tameka Empson, who had played the hilarious black neighbour from hell in *Beautiful Thing*, the 1996 box-office-hit film directed by Hettie MacDonald. After all, 'I've never considered acting as a career; I never thought I had it in me. At school, I was always the slightly tragic one at the back of the class who got asked last to play something like a tree. In one play, I played the wind and had to run up and down the aisles, so I gave it some welly, but it wasn't that in-depth.'

Being chosen to play Sam, Davina says, was perhaps fortunate 'as for me Sam is fairly similar to myself. She is very enthusiastic about life. She sees it as a game and is a terrible flirt, which I definitely am. She's quite a tomboy, too. Although people might find me a bit enthusiastic all the time, Sam is a little bit up and down.'

Although she was only too aware of the pitfalls that a television presenter-turned-actress can go through, and whereas she was half-expecting some flak from the critics, she was still going to have a go at what she said was 'venturing into something I haven't trained for. And people are naturally and understandably going to say, what gives her the right to become an actress? But it's up to them to judge whether I am any good or not. But I wouldn't have accepted the series if I hadn't been able to watch the pilot, and at the end of the day say, "That's OK" and not be hiding behind the sofa with a cushion over my eyes.'

Besides, she continued, 'it was a complete departure into the unknown. Sure I was petrified about learning the lines, but all the other cast members were so helpful in going through scenes.' So she felt a lot easier when the time came to record it in front of a live audience – well, sort of. That part wasn't so good, as far as she was concerned. In fact, she considered it easily as scary as any of her high-rise antics on *Don't Try This At Home*. On *Sam's Game*, 'we went to meet the audience before each show and it was absolutely terrifying. Never mind childbirth, if ever I needed a blast of oxygen from a face-mask, it was right then.'

And was she at all concerned about overexposure on TV? Apart from *Sam's Game*, she was also hosting *Big Brother* and *Don't Try This At Home*. Not that it seemed to bother her in the slightest. 'I'm not worried about the shows being on at the same time. They are all entirely different shows on different channels. But it's like buses, isn't it? I'm not on for six months, then suddenly I am on three times a week; it's a nightmare. I record my programmes throughout the year but if the television companies choose to put them on at the same time there is not much I can do about it.'

Nor could she do much about how folk would react to *Sam's Game*. Even though, 'I've never been cast as the leading lady, I just thought I had to give it my best shot.' And she repeated, 'If I felt I had to hide behind the sofa when I watched it, that would be the end of it – but I thought the pilot went quite well.' But she needn't have worried. In fact, she seemed more worried about husband Matthew. He appeared briefly in another episode, which completely threw Davina off balance. If it hadn't been for her, he probably wouldn't have even been in the programme. What happened, she recalls, is that 'the producer Sue was looking for a guy to play a small role at the end of an episode. So I volunteered Matthew, phoned him up and he said "yes" without thinking, and then realised it was a rugby day. So he wasn't best pleased.'

Not only that, but, as far as Davina was concerned, having to work with him was a nerve-racking experience. If there was one person she wanted to impress with her first attempt at acting, it was Matthew. And that probably came from the fact that, whenever he was at a recording, he had to stay out of sight: 'I always get very nervous if he's around me when I'm working, just because I want to be fantastic.' So one can only imagine what she must have been going through when they ended up in the same programme together. It was no different when he just went along as a member of the audience. Nine times out of ten, he had to be backstage. 'If he was out front I'd just focus on him. Then I couldn't concentrate until I found him. After that, I wouldn't be able to concentrate because I was looking at him. He had to be taken out of the audience once at a recording of *Don't Try This At Home* because I was fluffing my lines so badly.'

Looking back to the first episode of *Sam's Game*, however, and judging on first appearances, so to speak, it would probably be correct that not all reviewers shared the same thoughts as those of reviewer Steve Bennett. In fact, there were a few critics who considered viewers would soon be laughing along with what they were watching on screen. Especially when Davina's character Sam and her flatmate Alex throw a party, and the sleeping arrangements get confused and Alex wakes up in Sam's bed. Everybody gets the wrong idea, including

Phil, and their friend Marcia. And, of course, almost predictably for any farce, the climactic scene is when a naked Alex is discovered in Sam's bedroom with her lipstick smeared all over his nipples.

Probably the only justified criticism would be that, when Davina first appears on the screen, it's hard to see her as Sam rather than herself. But, as she pointed out, they do share a lot in common. 'Sam can be very feminine when she wants to be. But I'm not just being me; I could be feeling tired when Sam is feeling exuberant. In that sense, I did draw from somewhere else. She's not monotone; people might find me a little over enthusiastic, but she has lots of different colours. I am probably a bit more insecure than Sam. She's the sort of person I'd quite like to be, except that she'd probably quite like to be me, married and pregnant.'

But she still remembered that first day as the most frightening thing she has ever done. 'I was terrified, especially when we all went out to explain our characters to the audience. But I felt they were so behind us they were willing us to do well.' Being pregnant at the time didn't help matters either, but she stumbled across the perfect cure for morning sickness on the set. 'I was feeling a bit ill during filming. In one of the shows I had lots of cream crackers in my drawer and they are fantastic for morning sickness. So I had my face in the crackers all day and felt much better.'

She also developed some of the other expectant mother cravings – Coca-Cola was one of them. 'It's supposed to be really bad for you but all I want to do is drink gallons of it. And I've got to have the full-fat variety. It makes you feel better somehow when you are feeling a little sick.' And, like most mums-to-be, she did feel a little sick and had done for the first three months. 'So it's sex and Coca-Cola all day,' laughed Davina. Although Matthew undoubtedly benefited from her lusty ways, he put his foot down when it came to her sweet tooth. He 'won't let me eat sweets with any colour in either, so I have to go on a secret mission. My sister lives with us and she keeps them hidden under her bed for me.' Perhaps people forget that just because she is a celebrity it doesn't mean she does things any differently to anybody else. And, probably just to get the press going, she again confessed to feeling *that* something else: 'You go from feeling really dreadful to feeling really frisky – it's fantastic.'

Sam's Game premièred to mostly terrible reviews and, although most critics praised Davina's acting, for which she was nominated for a National Television Award in the plethora of award shows with which British television now abounds, the programme was no less savaged. Davina took it in her stride. 'If I feel good about what I've done, and I do, and if everyone thinks it's a pile of doo-doo, it won't matter.' In her eyes, she had done the best she could.

It couldn't have been that bad, nor could any of the other things she had done over the past 18 months or so. In addition to the nomination for Best Comedy, she was also up for another four gongs for Most Popular Comedy Presenter, Most Popular Entertainment Presenter, Most Popular Factual Programme and Most Popular Entertainment Programme. But *Sam's Game* winning would have turned one critic to despair. In his mind, 'It says a lot about the state of TV comedy today when a joke about someone being sick in the cutlery drawer is considered to be so hilarious it is thrown up a number of times.' Another added, 'It's the sort of thing she shouldn't have tried even at home, let alone on primetime TV.'

The viewing public had been equally unimpressed, and ratings for the show, which was shunted around the schedules, dropped from an initial 5.7 million viewers (25 per cent of the audience) to 2.2 million viewers (12 per cent) in its final week. A spokesman for ITV said, 'No decision has been made about *Sam's Game* yet and none is due for a couple of months.' And, although billed as Davina's breakthrough as an actress, it didn't take too much working out that it wasn't going to get past its first series. It wasn't long before the channel conceded that, having been panned by the critics and ignored by viewers, the sitcom would indeed be axed. Insiders had predicted much the same before it was officially announced. Most were convinced the show would not return for a second series, and they were right. That didn't stop Davina speaking out in defence of her decision to accept the role. 'It was tough, but I wouldn't have done it if I didn't think I could carry it off. I'm not saying I'm fantastic, but I'm not bad. Some will probably be happy to see me fall flat on my face, but that's up to them.'

Davina had more on her mind than whether or not she made a good actress, and whether she had fallen flat on her face in the eyes of the public and her critics: she was making plans for her own future. Among them was her decision to quit *Don't Try This At Home*. Yes, she announced, it would be her last series, she was certain about that. But she was still delighted that the series had achieved the fame of being featured in Alistair McGowan's *Big Impression*. 'It's the highest form of flattery,' she laughed. She also laughed, or rather dissolved into a bout of the giggles at the suggestion from a journalist that she might now be thinking of doing a rural Jamie Oliver act. How very homely, she thought, how very different from the all-action daredevil Davina clad in those hip-hugging leather trousers that we had all got used to see her cavorting about in on *Don't Try This At Home*. Once she and her husband Matthew became parents, she declared, there would be no more hair-raising escapades like the time she drove a mini-Moke across two steel girders fixed between a pair of 300-ft-high cliffs 'It's time to take on responsibility,' she said. 'I have to be more careful. I already do things very much with Matthew in mind, but around September there's a new person to consider. I won't even go bike riding now, with baby on the way. I can't do it any more because of Baby Robertson. Can you imagine me hanging out of a helicopter, or doing some other dangerous stunt when I was pregnant? Every week I did that show, it was like committing suicide. I've been so terrified and I don't want to feel scared any more. Having a baby to think about has taken the edge off my bravery. I have someone else to take care of now and it wouldn't be right doing all those things. I have had some great times, but it is right to move on.'

Certainly, being pregnant changed Davina's outlook on life. And who can blame her? That's why she decided she had to say goodbye to another series of *Don't Try This At Home*. But, while she said she would miss the team, she wouldn't miss the stunts. It was part of her contract that she had to take over any dare which a competitor refused, no matter how daunting. 'At times it was terrifying. For a start, I'm truly scared of heights, and often I felt like an idiot. And my insurance bills were pretty hefty, too.' Sure, she was sad that it was over but she was looking forward to challenges that might be just as demanding. For a moment, she seemed to be dreaming again of that house in the country and that family tugging at her apron strings.

She also vowed to take time off to bring up her baby. Despite outward appearances, she has always placed more value on her private life than on her work. 'I've never had any career game plan. In my personal life I've always wanted to get married, live in the country, keep ponies and Vietnamese pot-bellied pigs and have children tugging on my dress. But in my work I've just put one foot in front of the other and picked shows I felt I'd enjoy.' And, in answer to all the questions being thrown at her at the time: 'We definitely don't know the sex of the baby. I hate surprises, but Matthew tells me that that is one of life's great surprises, so I'm going to go with him on that one.'

So, was she definite about taking time off when baby arrived? 'Of course – probably about four months, I would think, which will take me well into 2002. After that, I'll probably employ a team of about four nannies, and then Hollywood beckons. Hey, look, I am joking. Who knows what's going to happen that far ahead? I have the feeling that doing television shows is a bit like waiting for the number 33 bus. You do a few of them, all nicely spaced out over a year or so, and then the network schedulers get to work and they all come along at once. The net result of which is the cry from the viewers of: "Oh, God, it's that McCall woman again!", which is perfectly understandable.'

However, with three shows more or less broadcasting at the same time, or at least within weeks of each other, she had been very much in viewers' faces and that was the one thing she didn't want. Despite her understanding that such things were very much in the hands of the programmers, she didn't want viewers to become tired of seeing too much of her. Like any other presenter, she was only too aware of the dangers of over exposure. That's why, 'I took three months off last year just because I thought you'd all had enough of me. There is a point when people go, "Get off the telly, she's a nightmare!"'

In 2001, she was, without question, TV's golden girl, and perhaps she was already worried that she might head down the same road as so many other golden presenters of television, who suddenly drop from favour and disappear into television oblivion.

Meanwhile, despite a busy summer with the return of *Big Brother*, she and Matthew were preparing for the birth of their baby. Her half-sister Caroline was already living with the couple. It was a set-up that sounded as if it could have come straight out of *Sam's Game*, but Davina insisted it was all very harmonious. 'I go and get into bed with Caroline in the morning and we watch breakfast television with our dogs, who aren't allowed into our bedroom because of Matthew's asthma. There's a secret for you,' she laughed. 'Caroline is going to carry on living with us once the baby is born, or for as long as she can put up with a crying baby. I'm sure she'll want to move out. But she's fantastic, I love her.' She felt the same about her other half-sister Millie, but Millie didn't live with them. 'Yes,' she said proudly, 'I've got two sisters and they are my closest friends. They keep me grounded and,' she joked, 'both of them are rude to me all the time.'

9

TIME OUT

On a hot summer's Friday night in August 2001, the final of *Big Brother 2* reached its climax. Davina was eight months' pregnant and worried that she might go into premature labour. Just before the final evictions of housemates Helen and Brian, she clutched her bump and was clearly in some distress, even though she had a special ambulance team standing by in case the worst happened. The medics were on hand and ready to rush her off to a nearby hospital in London's East End, if need be.

She was wearing a tight black T-shirt emblazoned with the words 'Big Mutha' and her huge bump was clearly visible. Despite all of this, she seemed surprisingly agile as she ran around the *Big Brother* compound but by the end of the second hour-long show she looked drained. Even as she took excited *Big Brother* winner Brian across the bridge from the house, he asked her, 'How long have you got to go?'

'Not long now,' Davina replied, 'you nearly brought it on tonight.'

Almost six weeks later, Holly (and not Holly-Willow, as Davina has pointed out since) arrived in the world, just 11 days later than expected. The timing of Holly's due date coincided with the international tragedy of 9/11 when two planes flew into New York's World Trade Center and another hit the Pentagon in Washington, leaving untold numbers injured or dead and throwing both cities – and indeed, the whole of America – into chaos. The tragedy began at the height of a morning rush hour in North America's largest city when a hijacked American Airlines jet slammed into one tower of the 110-storey World Trade Center. As smoke and flames poured out of the building and rescue workers battled to save victims, a second plane hit the adjacent tower. The two towers soon collapsed. Huge clouds of smoke hung over Manhattan and the nearby Wall Street financial markets were shut down. A short time later, another plane struck the Pentagon, setting off a massive explosion and tearing a hole in one side of the building. Davina recalled, 'I was heavily pregnant,

watching the day's events unfold in bed, in floods of
tears, and wondering what kind of a world I was
bringing my child into. Then, on 20 September, Holly
decided she wanted out – world disaster or not – and
two days later she arrived.'

Born on 22 September 2001 at 10.05pm, at birth
Holly weighed 8lb 12oz. She was born at home in
Chiswick, West London after Davina had decided to
opt for a home birth. In a statement issued soon
afterwards, she said, 'We are all doing brilliantly and I
can't heap enough praise on my husband and midwives
Caroline Flint and Pam Wilde, because I couldn't have
done it without them. Giving birth to Holly was the
best experience of my life – well, apart from making
her,' which, rumour had it, was during a holiday the
couple had enjoyed the previous Christmas. 'I have
never felt so beautiful and loved,' she continued. 'And,
seconds after Holly popped out, Matthew and I were
talking about having another one!'

But, eight weeks afterwards, she wasn't feeling so
good. She felt fat and depressed. 'Quite honestly, I am
Cellulite City and I feel like a beached whale. I'm
giving myself an incredibly hard time about my body,
which is daft I know, but I can't help it. The more I
worry about it, the more I eat, so it's a vicious circle.
I'm even embarrassed about going to the gym – I feel
so yuck. The thought of tight Lycra sends shivers

down my spine.' Adding to her post-natal misery was the dread of being snapped by the paparazzi on holiday. 'I'm ripe for being photographed getting on and off my sun lounger with a massive wedgie, looking like I'm about to eclipse the sun. You may think I am over-reacting but the only reason I am petrified is due to my new jelly belly.' Not that she needed to worry. Five months later she had slimmed down quite naturally without having to knuckle down to a strenuous fitness routine.

Perhaps she should have been cutting back on her workload in the lead-up to the birth of her first child. Interestingly enough, her appearance on *Big Brother 2* had been brought forward to ensure she could host it all the way through to the end. However, while she was pregnant she had been filming a couple of new shows that were intended to be screened while she took her four months or so away from the screen.

The first new series that she filmed was *Closure* for BBC Choice, the then new digital channel of the 'greatest broadcasting organisation in Britain'. The show also featured former *Big Brother* contestant Anna Noble, who to this day remains a firm friend of Davina's, as her roving reporter. It started its nine-week run that October just weeks after baby Holly had been born. According to the advance information that programme makers put out to the press, *Closure* would see Davina playing agony aunt to sort out the troubles of the famous and public alike, who all had something they wanted to get off their chests and put behind them for good. Among those celebrities taking part and seeking help about their stormy relationships – and also, perhaps, having the chance to say sorry and gain 'closure' – were pop star Dane Bowers and groups Hear'Say and Blue. 'The great thing about it,' Davina excitedly said, 'is that you just don't know what's going to happen.' Would an apology be accepted or rejected, and would those under the spotlight get the opportunity to make amends and apologise for their wrongdoings? It all sounded a grand idea and completely original, or was it? Well, not really. The format had already been tried and tested, and more or less done to death in America, only over there it was called *Forgive & Forget with Mother Love*.

Another show was *Oblivious*, inspired by a long tradition of hidden camera television programmes going back to *Candid Camera*, but with a different angle and bonus. *Camera* first appeared on British screens in the 1960s. The show ran for seven years and was initially presented by the late Bob Monkhouse. It featured Jonathan Routh and Arthur Atkins as pranksters. In 1974, it briefly returned to the screens, that time hosted by Peter Dulay. The original *Candid Camera* involved scenarios where unwitting members of the public would find themselves in unusual situations, acted out by pranksters Routh and Atkins, in which the unbelievable becomes almost believable. The victim of the pranksters' reactions would be filmed by a concealed camera and at some stage the joke was finally revealed to them, when the victim would be told, 'Smile, you're on *Candid Camera!*'

Just like *Candid Camera*, Davina's *Oblivious* also used hidden cameras and actors to put unsuspecting members of the public to the test. The difference was that the contestants, secretly nominated by family or friends, would bank thousands of pounds every time they answered a quirky SOS from a stranger. But, if they snubbed the request, which could range from helping to solve a crossword puzzle to loaning their trousers, they lost out. They would only discover they had been taking part in the ITV show as they sat in the studio audience weeks later and were unmasked by Davina. Filming for the programme took place in Birmingham, Liverpool, Manchester, Cardiff and Essex.

Prior to its first outing on ITV, the show's researcher Abi Oke said, 'We think *Oblivious* is going to be a massive hit because there is nothing like it on TV at the moment. We have all been approached by strangers asking for help in the past [and] we plan to find and reward Good Samaritans by giving them big money every time they help out one of our actors. We can't give away what the SOS requests will be, but they will be wacky, challenging or just plain funny. And the best part of *Oblivious* is that the contestants will not know they have taken part until we invite them to the recording under some pretence when Davina will reveal they are the stars of the show. They will then learn if they have won or lost money.' To start off the show, they would be looking for Birmingham contestants 'who are bright and bubbly, and up for a laugh. *Oblivious* is a family show, so nominees can be children, their parents or grandparents, but they must not know they have been nominated. This programme is all about putting ordinary people to the test. We hope to show the majority will come to the aid of a stranger in their hour of need.'

But, when *Oblivious* was premièred, one critic in particular simply hated it. The morning after the show had first aired, he wrote that Davina 'should have stayed at home through embarrassment. Apart from accepting the job in the first place, the biggest mistake she made last night was in her choice of dress.' Don't get me wrong, pleaded Ian Hyland in his review in the *Mirror*, 'women who are seven months' pregnant can still be sexy. But someone should tell Davina that turning up in a big blue maternity dress that makes you look like Hattie Jacques is not a good idea. Sadly the dress wasn't big enough to hide the fact that the show's format – *Big Brother* meets *Game For A Laugh* meets *Mr & Mrs* – stinks.

'The premise is that the unsuspecting punters in the studio audience were secretly filmed weeks ago and are now asked cash questions about what they were doing. Aside from being really naff, this is also a bit of a con. Once they were filmed, they would have been invited on to the show and asked to give their permission for the film to be used – hardly that oblivious then. Davina explained that someone in the audience had already played the game – "but you don't know who you are, do you?" – looking at the glazed faces in the audience. I believed that last bit.

'The first hilarious game involved people on the streets being asked to remember who said, "Ooh, I could crush a grape." Watching it was even more painful than crushing "grapes" in the medical sense. Still, a few people won some money and I realised why Davina got this job – no one else could shout "you've won £500" so excitedly. At times, she sounded like Bonnie Langford on helium. The next game could have been based on Davina's own quest for TV domination: "Do you fancy being watched from the moment you wake up until you go to bed?" she yelled. This was followed by "the part of the show where our contestants don't know what's going on". You can add "our viewers" to that, Davina.

'A pub singer was asked music questions and when Davina asked him how he'd done he said "crap". For some reason this was bleeped out, which puzzled me because ITV happily let the rest of this "crap" through. Later a girl was filmed being approached by an old woman, who asked her to clean up some dog poo. Did she "scoop the poop"? asked Davina. Yes, she did. And boy, was she not the only one, Davina.'

Despite this condemnation, soon after Davina and Matthew moved into their new home in the Surrey countryside and just as Holly was almost eight months old, she turned down what most presenters would have considered a most lucrative offer of £3 million from Capital Radio. But she did have her reasons. She much preferred to spend the time with her baby daughter and husband in their rural retreat. Despite serious consideration, she turned it down all the same. It was just a case of what many a new mother would understand: you can't put a price on quality time spent with family. She had apparently been secretly approached by the powers-that-be at the London station amid fears that *Breakfast Show* host Chris Tarrant might leave – they were already thinking that Davina would be perfect after she made such a hit out of Tarrant's show when he was on holiday.

It had all started because Chris Tarrant's contract with Capital Radio was about to end the following year and there were already rumours that he might not renew. His breakfast show was London's most-listened-to station with more than 3 million tuning in every morning between 6am and 9am, and one he had been presenting for over 20 years, so was he really about to walk away from it? It seemed so. Today the *Breakfast Show* is hosted by Johnny Vaughan, best known for his unique style of presenting *The Big Breakfast* on Channel 4 from 1997 to 2001.

The commitment of a daily radio show, and certainly one with a start so early in the morning, would have disrupted Davina's family life more than she was prepared for: her priorities lay with Holly, her husband and her television career. She was far happier at the thought of working in television and seeing as much of her daughter and her husband as she could. At the end of the day, she simply did not want to swap the small screen for a daily radio show. Well, not long-term, anyway. Not only that but Davina was preparing to start filming a third series of *Big Brother* for Channel 4 two weeks after the offer was made in May 2002. Even if she had wanted the radio gig, it would have been impossible because she certainly would not have given up the one show she loved doing most. She also had other projects to which she was already committed, such as *The Vault* for ITV and another series of *Closure* for the BBC later that same year. There was also talk of Davina's wish for more children as soon as possible. Yes, she said, 'I hope to have loads more kids – being a mum puts work into perspective.' She was also enjoying the status of being Britain's most popular female TV presenter.

Not so good, a few months earlier in March 2002, and perhaps touching on the downside to being a celebrity, was the news that burglars had broken into Davina's home. They had gone into her bedroom and stolen her knickers. Making matters worse, on closer inspection, she discovered that jewellery, photographs and two mobile phones containing dozens of private numbers for celebrity friends were also missing. According to journalist Sean O'Brien, reporting the incident in the *People*, Davina was shaken that someone had been through all her things and she thought it was, to say the least, quite creepy that some of her underwear had gone as well. Like anyone who has ever been a victim of crime, such as burglary of personal possessions, she felt violated that complete strangers had been going through private items in her bedroom.

All the police could do, it seemed, was to link the break-in to builders who had been carrying out renovation work. As one of those ubiquitous 'insiders' said, 'The thieves weren't too bright about what they did with the mobiles. They were used to call the building firm that had been hired to do the work, so it was almost certain it was one of their men who had stolen Davina's stuff. But the problem for the police was that there were so many builders and sub-contractors on the job it would have been extremely difficult to discover exactly who was to blame. In the end, Davina and Matthew didn't think it was worth going ahead with the investigation, especially as the stolen items weren't that expensive.'

All the same, the couple became so concerned about their home security that they set up a Neighbourhood Watch Scheme. According to one neighbour, it was good that they did: 'The thefts from Davina's house really shook her up, especially because she has now got the security of her little girl to think about. Her husband Matthew was instrumental in setting up the Neighbourhood Watch Scheme and they are both very community-spirited. Now everybody keeps an eye out for them to make sure this sort of thing doesn't happen again.'

The same community spirit was once more in evidence just a few months after Davina turned down the offer from Capital Radio when she put on her protest hat over an issue she felt most strongly about. When she moved from Chiswick to Surrey, one of the hopes she had was to swap London life for a low-key alternative with sweeping views, fresh air and a healthy environment in which to raise her baby daughter. But she was outraged to learn only eight months after moving into her new home that a mobile phone company wanted to erect a 75-foot radio mast just yards from her property. Dreading possible side-effects to the health of her baby and incensed at the blemish on her chosen landscape, Davina joined protesters and fired off a series of letters to planners. She said she was 'worried sick' about the possible effects on her now 10-month-old daughter Holly. She was unable to sleep or concentrate at work, and thought that moving on again was the only answer.

After a high-profile planning battle, O2 (who, interestingly enough, was the sponsor of *Big Brother* at the time) dropped plans for the development. 'We would be horrified to live next to such a monstrosity,' complained Davina in a first letter to planners. 'The potential health risks are not yet known and we have a 10-month-old baby. Please, please find somewhere else to put this mast. It should *not* be in such a beautiful residential area. This antenna would be a horrendous eyesore for both us and the general public who enjoy the area. A bridleway runs right next to it, which is often used by walkers, riders and pedestrians. It would ruin a beautiful scenic walk. Instead of looking at the amazing countryside, walkers would be faced with a 25-metre aerial.'

After inspecting detailed plans for the proposed development in Woldingham, Surrey, Davina wrote a second letter to planners at Tandridge Borough Council. 'The mast is enormous, as is its compound and fence. I understand that we are not allowed to argue on health grounds. However, my husband and I are worried sick about the perceived health threat to our 10-month-old baby girl. If the government decrees that these masts should not be built by a school, where children reside between 9am and 3pm, how can it be all right for our 10-month-old little girl to live 21 metres from it 24 hours a day? I cannot concentrate at work and am having trouble sleeping at night. This may not be your concern but, if this mast goes up, we would rather move than put our child at risk, which according to many websites is a very real danger.'

The mobile-phone company was well aware of her opposition, too. A company spokesman said, 'Miss McCall is a private citizen and she has a right to express her own views. We work within strict guidelines for building these masts and they are only put up to improve services for our customers.'

Soon after, O2 quietly dropped the proposals. It said existing masts could be upgraded to improve network coverage. Tandridge planning officer Piers Mason said, 'We received an email from O2 saying they no longer wanted to proceed with the situation. But they didn't give any reasons. We have now confirmed to them that we have withdrawn any applications regarding the mast. I am sure the local residents will be pleased.' And certainly they were. Vicky Barker was one of them. She lived at High Shaw House, the property that would have been closest to the mast, and she told reporters, 'We are all totally delighted. Everyone has been fighting hard against the plans and everyone was worried.'

But two years later it was to be Davina in the firing line, this time for advertising O2's competitor, Vodafone. Campaigners were less than happy about it. What happened was that Davina had been paid a reported 'fat fee' to help launch Vodafone's new range of trendy 3G phones in Dublin. Literally dozens more transmitting masts needed to be built all over Ireland to cope with the new network, which critics said could cause cancer and blood clots, especially in children. The hi-tech 3G – Third Generation – sets allow callers to see each other, look at videos and download the latest games. And making matters worse was the fanfare of publicity in which Davina was full of praise for the phones. 'I've got quite good at them, especially the Motorola ones,' she said.

Lisa Oldham, spokeswoman for pressure group

Mast Sanity, snapped, 'A lot of people will be very disappointed in her. These masts can hurt children – in Ireland or anywhere.' Irish campaigner Dr Don McCauley said much the same.

This was not the first time that Davina had been linked to Vodafone. In July 2002 she watched the British Grand Prix from the Vodafone hospitality tent at Silverstone. At the height of the debate, a Vodafone Ireland spokesman said, 'Davina was a pleasure to work with, and we were delighted with the resulting coverage.' Despite such uproar, there was no further comment from either Davina or from any of her representatives.

Clare Grant, writing in the *Daily Mirror*, noted in May 2002, there was a time when Davina was desperate for the fame and status she now enjoys as Britain's most popular female TV presenter. 'This month alone she fronts a new prime time ITV1 quiz show, *The Vault*, a third series of the phenomenally successful *Big Brother* for Channel 4, which starts on 24 May, and then she begins work on a second series of the BBC show *Closure*. Being so much in demand would once have been all she needed to make her life complete, but her priorities have changed.

'Davina now wants a different kind of attention, the sort of sticky-fingered, cuddly, demanding type that comes with a brood of happy children. And if that means her career being less high profile, or even coming to a temporary halt then so be it. She is prepared to sacrifice her hard-earned success to make sure her 8-month-old daughter Holly has lots of brothers and sisters to play with.'

Equally, Davina was also now pleased to be raising her daughter in a beautifully picturesque and idyllic part of the countryside. It was also providing a relaxing haven for her to escape to after work, especially with the hours she was then putting into rehearsing for *The Vault*, her latest and newest television game show. The idea behind this particular show was that wannabe contestants could register on a special phone line, from which seven would be picked to play for a top cash prize in the studio. They would have to guess the secret combination of *The Vault* – a strong room containing the £100,000 cash prize – before facing three rounds of general knowledge questions, all answered against the clock and holding a cash value. Finally, the remaining contestant had to answer 10 questions correctly to win.

If they failed, Davina would make a live phone call to a randomly selected number from the viewers' registration phone line. That viewer had to answer six questions correctly in one minute to win the jackpot. 'I've never done a show like this before,' she enthused. 'I love general knowledge quizzes – not that I'm any good at them, unlike my dad who wipes the board with everyone at Trivial Pursuit, but I love new challenges. It's a tense show, the kind where you end up shouting at the telly. The contestants are going to be very nervous because it's against the clock. As for me, the adrenalin of doing a live show is always intense. It takes hours to wind down. I used to get very, very nervous, but, as time has gone by, I'm able to relax more – I just get excited!'

Big Brother 3 was equally thrilling. According to fan Phil Lewin's account of the final night, it couldn't have been better. 'It's Friday, July 26, 2002, and the biggest day of the year for British reality-TV fans – the live *Big Brother* final. This is the equivalent of the Oscars or the Superbowl for public and media attention as millions of reality fans who have laughed, ogled or cringed at the 12 housemates for the last nine weeks finally avidly discover which one would be the last out of the house and walk away with the prize money. At £70,000 (roughly US $110,000), this is a pretty meagre sum compared with the first prize on *Survivor*, or even a reasonable run on *Who Wants to Be a Millionaire*. However, such is the enormity of *Big Brother* in the UK that the opportunities open to the winner, including media interviews, personal appearances and lucrative commercial deals, to say nothing of a potential career change, quickly dwarf the immediate prize money.

Although you don't necessarily have to be the winner to benefit, as the season-one rule-breaking "villain" Nick Bateman proved.'

On the night itself ten million viewers tuned into Channel 4, while hundreds more, lucky enough to get tickets, filled the set beside the *Big Brother* house at Elstree. Davina, dressed entirely in white, was on an equal high. She ran round stating that people in the crowd had travelled all the way from Australia and New Zealand, though these might have been backpackers passing through and keen to party along with the rest. Surely no one would be crazy enough to fly halfway round the world for the sake of a reality TV-show final, or would they?

The waiting crowd were wound up to fever pitch, but with good reason. *Big Brother*'s first two finals were between three people and of those realistically the winner was going to be one of two (Anna or Craig in season one and Helen or Brian in season two). This time any of the four housemates who remained – Jade, Alex, Jonny or Kate – remained in the running. Throughout the week opinion polls and betting odds fluctuated and the outcome of the evening's events was something no one could confidently predict.

Davina had a brief conversation with the four housemates' families and friends (through the series Jade's mother and Alex's parents, like their siblings, became cult figures in their own right) and then she opened the mike to the house. Having had a few glasses of wine to ease the tension (though wisely keeping off the punch after the week's earlier carnage), the final four cheered wildly. After the traditional long pause, Davina announced that the ninth person to leave the house would be Essex girl Jade. She screamed delightedly and, after adjusting her large breasts and hugging the others, walked up the stairs and out of the house, wearing a pretty pink dress with matching gloves. With her hair slung seductively over her right eye, she looked amazing. It was such a contrast to three weeks ago when pig references were at their height. At the time it was expected that Jade would have been almost lynched, had she left the house but that was then and now she received a rapturous reception. Men's underwear was thrown, and she kissed and hugged fans in the crowd, yelling ecstatically, 'You're all chipsticks!'

Davina was eventually able to drag her into the studio, where she was greeted by family and friends; also talk-show presenter Graham Norton, who like several tabloid newspapers and other pundits had originally rubbished her. However, he made a rapid U-turn when it was evident that the vilification of Jade had gone too far and instead turned her into a ballsy heroine. The role of *Big Brother* gay icon had seemingly always belonged to the lovely Alex, so this was totally unexpected. Jade was thrilled to be shown a clip of another celebrity fan, Johnny Depp (interviewed by Norton and at the time in London at work on the film version of JM Barrie's *Neverland*), who condemned the abuse she was getting.

Davina went on to show Jade a montage of bitching, which brought her back to reality. She was at pains to explain that she had always attempted to be honest to people's faces (she wasn't, especially to Sophie) and she said Adele had upset her by repeating her comments in an effort to turn others against her. But more importantly in people's minds was an admission of the nature of the 'sex act' with PJ, who previously denied anything had happened. As this was before the 9pm watershed, Jade had to curtail her description of the act. With intrigue building, she ringed one of the various options listed on a card, seemingly unembarrassed by a replay of the footage. At this point Davina promised the audience that everything would be revealed after 9pm, which is when all minors watching are supposed to be safely tucked up in bed.

However, such sensitivities did not prevent Jade being shown selected highlights of the nude scene (bar the kebab) at which she cringed still further. Summing up, we were treated to a collection of Jadisms: Mr

Heinstein, East Angular and all. Sensing everyone's curiosity, Davina asked Jade what she had learned from life in the house to which she replied, 'Chickens don't eat cheese.' What a fantastic epitaph!

Half an hour later Davina revealed the tenth person to leave the house. This time Alex shook hands and hugged his housemates then put on the same leather jacket he wore to enter the house and coolly strutted out. As fans chanted his name, he waved happily. Reunited with family and friends, he was so emotional that it was some time before Davina could get close to him for a few words. Eventually he gave an insightful interview into how life in the *Big Brother* house had impacted on him. He had got on well with Sandy and Adele; also enjoyed 'following the van' with Kate, though that trip was now well and truly over. Davina then showed him a clip of Adele admitting she 'fancied the arse off him'. He stated that he would see her again, though he was non-committal about future developments.

Alex's interview ended with a montage of his most drunken moments, including his widely acclaimed bedroom rendition of 'That's the Way I Like It.'

Two contestants remained in the house but it was no surprise to anyone that the last two housemates happened to be the most public performers. Throughout the series, Kate and Jonny had equally enlivened (and antagonised) housemates and cameras with their bad jokes, silly games, impersonations and continual flirting, albeit platonic. They seemed to have struck up a fantastic friendship, one that might possibly be longer lasting than any of the other relationships developed in the house that year. But now they were sweetly embracing on the sofa and attempting to persuade the other that they would win.

Keeping up the tension, Davina brought the majority of the other housemates onstage. First up, Lynne and Spencer (for once not arguing). In the crowd girls screamed in delight to see 'Spanky' again. Evicted five weeks ago, his fans remained convinced he was the moral winner. Then came 'lurve god' Lee holding hands with Adele and Sophie, the latter clinging on in triumph. Alison and a strutting PJ appeared, followed by Jade, Alex and Tim (who was roundly booed). Sunita made an appearance and said how good it was to finally meet Davina (a privilege denied anyone leaving the house of their own accord). The 'enigmatic' Sandy (Davina's description) was the only housemate missing. In fact, he is reported as saying that he disliked some of his housemates so much he couldn't bear to go near them again, his least favourites being Jonny and Kate. As a stand-in, the puppet produced by housemates earlier was introduced.

It was then the moment half the country had been waiting for: when Davina spoke to the house. The picture from within promptly disappeared and a few hearts in the production team must have missed beats at this point. But seconds later Jonny and Kate reappeared on the big screen, nervously holding hands on the sofa. There was a long pause and then Davina declared Kate the winner.

Naturally, this moment is usually the most emotional of the whole *Big Brother* series, but this time scenes in the house were truly amazing. Despite confidently predicting at the start of the series that she wanted to be the first woman to win *Big Brother*, the outcome was obviously a genuine surprise to Kate. A look of complete incredulity came over her face but soon she and Jonny collapsed into one noisy, hysterical heap. Endearingly, Jonny seemed genuinely thrilled for Kate, who by now was in floods of tears. Outside the waiting crowd went wild at what was clearly a popular decision (with three million votes being cast for Kate against two and a quarter million for Jonny in the end the margin was pretty decisive). Now it was Jonny's turn to leave the house. After one last hug, he left to a rapturous reception, with more chanting of his name while his fire station colleagues from the North East waved around yellow plastic hats (Davina wore one in tribute). Laughing and waving, he made his way to the studio to be greeted by his family and girlfriend Joanne.

What followed must be one of the finest pieces of surreal television of all time, again courtesy of Graham Norton. Dustin Hoffman appeared in a sketch featuring 'Jonny' in the *Big Brother* diary room, wearing his fireman's helmet and clutching a large bottle of cider, growling miserably about how drunk he was and about his numerous nominations for eviction.

Once the excitement had died down a little, Jonny discussed his more dubious hygiene habits (though he was now reconciled with Alex) and his love of displaying his backside. A montage of mooning followed, including to *Big Brother* in the Diary Room. Davina asked him about his disagreement with Sandy, who had already said quite publicly that he disliked Jonny, the incident sparking off Sandy's gradual paranoia. Jonny told the audience what he would have said to Sandy, had they been outside the house, 'F**k off, you boring Scottish bastard!' When Davina questioned him as to Alex and Adele's suggestion that he was playing up to the cameras, Jonny admitted he had found it hard to ignore the fact that he was on television. He said that the real Jonny was the stupid one, but pressures within the house had brought out his more serious side.

However, PJ, Alison and Kate had helped him through the bad times. Affectionately he declared, 'Kate is an idiot.' Davina went on to show Alex's best moment: hiding under a blanket to steal chocolate from the 'rich' side of the house while the bars were up. Summing up his time in the house Jonny said he wanted to be remembered as 'the guy who put a smile on the nation's face.'

Beside herself with excitement (and accidentally referring to the 'final of *Big Brother* 2001'), Davina went back outside to greet Kate, the overall winner. But before that interview could take place there was the explanation of the Jade/PJ sex act, which could not be described on air until after 9pm. Davina held up the card, which Jade had already filled in, indicating that a 'hand job' had occurred, whereupon the crowd cheered wildly. Of course some may have hoped for something a little more risqué and were no doubt disappointed. Later one Sunday tabloid attempted to claim Jade had subsequently admitted after the show that a blow job had taken place, but it would seem the whole truth will never be revealed.

After Jonny left the house, Kate lay prostrate on the sofa for several minutes, presumably in shock. She then sat up with her head in her hands. Slightly gaining composure, she helped herself to the last of the punch and attempted to wipe away her tears, her make-up now badly smudged. Meanwhile, Davina entered the house to congratulate the winner of that year's *Big Brother*, saying, 'Kate, you're the first woman ever to win *Big Brother*, how do you feel?' Beside herself, Kate wailed, 'I've shit myself, it's so fantastic!' before offering Davina a drink. With little to say in response, Davina persuaded Kate to do her impersonation of herself and Kate soon returned to her normal, perky self.

Kate, too, had attracted the attention of another celebrity. This time it was Duncan James from Brit boy band Blue, who said hello and promised to come over for drinks after their gig in Essex that night. He also wanted to text her. After just a few minutes, Kate had a potential celebrity boyfriend – not bad going. Naturally Davina went on to focus on Kate's many and varied flirtations during her time in the house. First, how did she feel about Spanky (Spencer)? Kate conceded she did fancy him, but went on to say, forgetting Tim, that she also fancied all the other male housemates except Sandy and Lee. Contrary to tabloid rumour, she said that she did not 'fumble' Spencer, but he was the one doing the fumbling. And as if being attracted to four men wasn't enough, Davina then raised the matter of Kate's kiss with Adele. Kate claimed this was just a kiss and not a 'romp'. Davina went on to ask about 'Follow the van' and where the van was parked. To which Kate replied, 'Nowhere, apart from Adele's nipple.'

A montage of Kate's finest (mostly drunken) moments followed, finishing with her slapstick attempts to remove a pair of trousers and falling down in the process. Davina questioned her on her hopes for the future. Modestly she replied, 'I don't know.' It was obvious, though, that she was not going to be short of choices. As a parting *Big Brother* gift, Davina gave Kate a pair of Gucci sunglasses to replace the ones she broke while living on the 'poor' side of the house.

Amid more emotional and joyous scenes, Kate left the house. It might have been the opening of the Olympic Games as fireworks exploded and the crowds cheered themselves hoarse. Kate appeared on stage to embrace her close-knit family and circle of friends, followed by her fellow housemates. A graphic of £70,000 being transferred to Kate's account was shown on the big screen, though Kate herself was more concerned about the accompanying photograph. After more fireworks, Kate kissed Spencer and was thrown around by her mate Jonny. Away from the crowds, the lights in the house went out. Sixty-four days later and it was finally the end of *Big Brother* 2002.

10

ONE MORE TIME

The news, when it came, was totally unexpected. In January 2003, it was announced that Davina would replace Matthew Kelly as host of *Stars In Their Eyes* to present three celebrity editions that would go out as *Coronation Street*, *Soap Stars* and *Legends* specials over three consecutive weeks in February of that year. She would be billed as a guest presenter and would be acting caretaker of the show while Kelly's future in television lay very much in question.

Matthew Kelly was being held by police in connection with alleged sexual abuse against a boy, who was under 16 years of age. In a statement released on his behalf by London-based law firm Kingsley Napley, the star said the accusation was not true: 'Mr Kelly emphatically denies the allegation made against him which has come as a complete shock and surprise. He has co-operated fully today with the police and will of course continue to do so, should that be necessary. It should be noted that he has been released without charge.' Indeed, the matter did not proceed any further and he was never charged.

Stars In Their Eyes debuted on ITV as a series of 30-minute shows in July 1990, which was then presented by Leslie Crowther. But, when Crowther was severely injured in a road accident in 1992, he was replaced by Kelly, who never missed a show apart from the odd occasion when Russ Abbott hosted a one-off Elvis Presley special, for example, and of course now for more serious reasons. First and foremost, the show was a programme about tension building up by filming the contestants at home or work before chatting to the host, and then disappearing through the Star Door to reappear seconds later in a cloud of dry ice as the star they would be mimicking. The studio audience was legally obliged to applaud after a few bars of the song. And, like so many shows of the period and since, each series culminated in a live final, in which viewers voted for their favourite performer.

It is interesting to note perhaps that among the most impersonated stars were Elvis Presley, Cliff Richard, Cher, George Michael and Madonna. During its peak run when Kelly hosted the show, *Stars In Their Eyes* attracted a record number of applicants. The series screened five years before Kelly's arrest, for instance, had 50,000 applicants for the 60 places that were available. Needless to say the programme went on to be named the Most Popular Entertainment Show at the National Television Awards in each of the four years it was nominated. Of course, there had been other celebrity editions of the show, and perhaps none as intriguing as when the first was shown in 1998 when, perhaps for the first time on national television, a show had been dedicated to celebrities who wanted to become another celebrity. It was very much in the same vein as what Pete Waterman had observed about Kylie Minogue back in the early nineties that everyone wanted to be Kylie, except Kylie who wanted to be Madonna.

The former manager of seventies pop band The Bay City Rollers, Tam Paton, had also been arrested at the same time as Kelly in connection with the same inquiry, but no charges were made and the inquiry was dropped. Both had been detained as part of the sex-abuse inquiry that led to the conviction of pop mogul Jonathan King. He was found guilty of four indecent assaults and two serious sexual offences against boys carried out in the 1980s, for which he was registered as a sex offender and banned from working with children. Although one or two questioned whether the police were carrying out a celebrity witch-hunt, the police were quick to deny it. The accusation had come amid reports that other famous people were being investigated. But Surrey Police insisted their investigation focused on specific allegations and was not a 'wide-ranging trawl into the showbusiness world'. A spokesman added that the recent arrests were not part of Operation Ore, the investigation into users of a US child-pornography website. It was believed at the time that accusations all dated from the 1970s, and that the inquiry had been ongoing for several months at that stage.

Kelly was arrested at the Birmingham Repertory Theatre, where he was appearing in pantomime as Captain Hook in a production of *Peter Pan*. In a statement the day after his arrest, and after he had temporarily dropped out of the show, the theatre said the pantomime would continue without him. Although the married father with two grown-up children of his own returned to the pantomime after police were through with their questioning, the result of talks between Kelly's agent and Nigel Hall, then Granada TV's controller of entertainment, was not such good news. It was decided that in the circumstances it would perhaps be best if he did not present the three celebrity editions of *Stars In Their*

Eyes. At that time Davina was asked to step in and take over until the matter had been cleared up and resolved, for better or worse.

Both Granada and ITV said they were fully in support of Kelly, who emphatically denied the allegation, and in the end no charge was brought against him.

Of course, it then turned into a media circus in much the same way as Winona Ryder's shoplifting trial had done a year or so before. There is still much speculation as to whether Ryder was simply being used as a warning to other celebrities in Beverly Hills that might be thinking of doing the same thing. Many of Ryder's supporters would argue that she was a victim of example. However, the message, loud and clear, from Saks Fifth Avenue was that, star or not, they were not going to tolerate any shoplifting.

Filming of the celebrity *Stars In Their Eyes* went ahead as planned with Davina presenting. 'I've huge respect for Davina,' said Kelly, 'and know she will do a terrific job caretaking the show.' But, according to ITV insiders, bosses were still playing everything very much by ear, and would be waiting for the outcome of police enquiries before deciding what to do next. Or even whether they would proceed with a then unseen series of *Stars In Their Eyes* recorded the previous September. There was even talk of scrapping any further episodes of the show featuring children emulating their pop idols.

Kelly was released on bail until 12 March by Surrey Police 'pending further investigation', he continued to reject the accusations that he abused underage boys in the 1970s. When he returned to walk back on to the stage of *Peter Pan*, it was clear from the thunderous applause he received from the entire audience that no one doubted that he was indeed innocent. It was only while he was treading the boards in Birmingham that his television career looked as if it was in jeopardy, or at least for the time being, despite growing support for his innocence from every quarter imaginable. Perhaps the most surprising support, though, came from Jonathan King, who had always claimed he had been the victim of false allegations himself. Despite having never met Kelly, he still wanted to speak out in his defence.

In a posting on his website, King announced, 'I don't think I've ever met Matthew Kelly, but I wish him the best in his battle against a media starving for celebrity targets.' In a reference to the *Stars In Their Eyes* catchphrase, King added, 'If he fails, I'd say to him, "Tonight, Matthew, you've been, like me, a victim of false allegations – the current growth area of British injustice."'

Davina was pleased to have helped simply by

standing in for Kelly. During one of the breaks in recording of the celebrity specials, she told the audience at Manchester's Granada Studios how nervous she was about presenting the show. 'This is an honour for me as this is Matthew's show. I have watched *Stars In Their Eyes* for years. I love this show, but I am merely standing in for Matthew.' The audience totally backed Davina's sentiments, as did ITV's Nigel Hall. They were cheering and some even wept at the support being shown for Kelly.

In the same month as the celebrity *Stars In Their Eyes* recorded shows were broadcast, Davina found herself presenting the Brit Awards, the most anticipated night in the music industry calendar. By the time she was brought in to host the event on 20 February 2003, the show had gained a reputation for being entertaining for all the wrong reasons. In 1992 the band KLF fired blanks from a machine gun, while in 1996 Pulp frontman Jarvis Cocker was arrested for jumping on stage and turning his bottom to the audience during a performance by Michael Jackson. Then in 1998 a member of Chumbawumba poured a bucket of ice over an unsuspecting John Prescott. And now, in 2003, the aim was that music, not embarrassing incidents, should make the headlines. So in came Davina ready to save the day, only according to Jo Wiltshire writing in the *Mail On Sunday*, one week after the event, she didn't: 'Her ad libs and trademark down-to-earth quips didn't quite come off and she seemed uncertain for much of the show.' Afterwards Davina seemed eager to return to her husband, sitting at the back of the audience, for a few minutes of what seemed to be reassuring hugs.

In her defence, the majority view was that circumstances seemed to be against her. For this particular Brits cramped theatre seating replaced the traditional boozy tables (no alcohol was available until the after-show party). For once, aside from those in the 'pit', most of the audience remained firmly seated (alcohol-fuelled dancing being the norm). Many celebrities left early, while others, including award-winners Eminem, Robbie Williams and the Red Hot Chili Peppers seemingly unconcerned about making an appearance.

Perhaps this was all too much for Davina to turn round. Maybe the organisers should have realised that the whole point of an awards show like the Brits is that there's always the slight chance dangling that something might go wrong. As a nation, we crave misbehaviour. On this occasion Justin Timberlake grabbing Princess Kylie's by now ubiquitous derrière while the pair duetted on their rendition of Blondie's 'Rapture' was not enough to bring the house down.

Less than one month after the Brit Awards at Earls

Court, and while the Kelly investigation still rolled on, another new show, *Reborn In The USA*, that turned up trumps for Davina was about to hit the screens. Ten former British pop acts (such as Spandau Ballet's vocalist Tony Hadley, Go West's Peter Cox, Elkie Brooks, Sonia and Gina G, all of whom were more or less unknown in the USA) were bussed from coast to coast – from Detroit to Memphis – with a number of lesser stars, in a bid to see if they could revitalise their music careers. Memphis, of course, was where the legendary Sun Studio was located, and where Elvis Presley had made his first records – and, perhaps more importantly, where Graceland was also situated. Named after Grace Toof, the original owner's aunt, this was the home Elvis had bought in 1957, the year he made his first million, and from all accounts he periodically had it redecorated and refurbished according to his notoriously kitsch tastes. Interestingly enough, it was Elkie Brooks, still one of Britain's finest female singers of the last half-century, who had won critical acclaim for her remarkable bluesy performance of 'A Mess of Blues' (one of Presley's first and best post-army recordings from 1960) on an ITV tribute show in the year following Presley's untimely death in 1977. Each week, the American audience voted for their favourite act. The two acts with the fewest votes would then face the vote from the British public, and the following week the act with the fewest votes was eliminated from the contest, got off the bus and was sent back to Britain.

Detroit was in fact the opening city of the tour and the TV show, and where better, Davina thought, to announce the news that she was three months' pregnant with her second child to a live audience, viewers, crew and the eight acts. She even joked about her condition: 'In case you lot at home had been thinking I'd been hitting the Dunkin' Donuts, or had some sort of breast enhancement, I am actually pregnant.'

As with the birth of Holly 18 months earlier, she was thrilled to pieces. 'Being a mum is the best thing that's happened to me. I think two-and-a-half or three years is a good age gap between children. Of course, it's mad, saying when you want to get pregnant at a certain time – you can never predict what will happen. I want to take a couple of months off work so Matthew and I can go away somewhere, maybe Australia. My age is a factor but lots of women leave having babies until they're older now. People I know are having kids at my age because, like me, they wanted to do different things in their twenties. After 35 doctors suggest having tests to make sure everything is OK. With the tests comes the chance of miscarriage, so I don't want to leave it too late.'

All the same, with or without Davina being

pregnant, there was many a critic who had almost been dreading the start of the series in what some unnecessarily and negatively described as 'let's try and make these has-beens famous again', and even worse was the presenter. Yes, noted Paddy Shannan writing in the *Liverpool Echo*, it is 'once again, Davina McCall, the queen of primetime tat, who will be adopting that inane grin, putting on that silly girlie voice and pulling those ridiculous faces'. But was it really that bad? Not according to Elkie Brooks: 'I treated *Reborn* as a personal challenge. Prior to being accepted on the show, I had been rejected three times for having too much to say on a musical level. Rejection made me want it more and, having always wanted to go on a musical pilgrimage of America, this seemed like the perfect opportunity to do just that, and getting paid for something you've always wanted to do isn't bad going.' If there was anything wrong about it, she continued, it was that 'we were led to believe that music was the essence of the show. But when the idea of the live band was replaced with backing tracks it became clear that music wasn't the priority, and I'm not sure that any of us would have considered taking part if it had meant compromising to the level we did. It is a shame because the show had great potential. Despite that, I'm always up for trying new things, and as well as forming new friendships I have had nothing but a positive response since then.'

As for Davina? 'She was pregnant at the time and I'll always be amazed at how she devoured a hamburger with such gusto – I have never known anyone to eat a burger so fast! Though I never got to know Davina personally, I saw a confident, attractive woman who knows exactly what she's about. She is very professional and just gets on with her job; I would say we were pretty similar like that. It's always refreshing to see a strong woman in a typically male profession. I don't know what she thought of the show, or me – or the others for that matter, but I'm certain that she has a long and successful future ahead of her.' And, of course, she was right.

Also correct, in some ways but not all, was an amusing overview of the show that appeared on the internet during the run of the series. Like so many, it questioned, quite cynically, why becoming famous was now a lot like becoming king or queen: 'It requires a lot of luck. Luck of birth, whether in bloodline or talent, followed by years of strict belief in destiny rather than getting a proper job. Plus, the power struggle isn't over once you reign supreme: soon enough you're overpampered and paranoid about losing the throne. But times change. The old order passes in favour of the new, and now fame is starting to look more like a series of elections. *American Idol*

Davina during the 25th Brit Awards at Earl's Court in London 2005, embracing and kissing former *Don't Try This At Home* co-presenter Kate Thornton.

Davina has hosted an attended many award ceremonies. Here she is pictured with husband Matthew at the 2005 National Television Awards at the Royal Albert Hall (*top left*); on the red carpet at the Bafta Television Awards in April 2004, where she picked up 'The Most Popular Reality Programme' award for *Big Brother*; letting her hair down at *GQ* Men Of The Year awards in 2005. Davina has also presented the Brits, and is pictured clutching one of the coveted awards.

Davina McCall and David Coulthard aboard the Hugo Boss for the Open 60
Celebrity Boat Race during Cowes Week on the Isle Of Wight in August 2005.

Being pregnant didn't put Davina off the job! Here she is wearing her now famous 'Big Mutha' t-shirt while eight months pregnant during the *Big Brother 2* final in August 2001. It didn't take her long to slim down again, and in case there was any doubt, Davina bravely stripped down to a black bikini to interview *Big Brother* housemate Sam Heuston on her eviction during the sixth series in June 2005.

Top: Davina with Jade Goody during the *Big Brother 3* eviction night in July 2002, and Chantelle Houghton (*bottom*), the first non-celebrity to win a *Celebrity Big Brother* in January 2006. She is pictured here with Davina during the final.

Celebrity Big Brother. Davina is an expert in dealing with other celebrities, as she once again proved in *Celebrity Big Brother* 2006. Here she is pictured with (*Clockwise from top left*) Traci Bingham, Pete Burns and Michael Barrymore.

The real Davina with her waxwork at Madame Tussauds, in London on 16 Febrauary 2006, for the opening of the *Big Brother Experience*.

Davina as British TV viewers know her best … presenting, and looking stunning while she's at it!

resembles the bright-eyed, fiercely competitive campaign trail, and *I'm A Celebrity, Get Me Out Of Here!* feels conversely like a sort of impeachment.

'So what about those past big shots, voted in for a second term? Make room on the reality-TV bench for *Reborn In The USA*, a British show with an ingeniously cruel concept. A busload of UK chart-toppers tour seven US cities, each week gamely ripping off a song synonymous with the location from New Orleans blues in week one to Sinatra for a New York finale. The American audience votes on talent alone, presumably ignorant of the performers' notoriety back home. And that's the catch. They're washed up has-beens. Even in the UK, they're not famous any more.

'Not great news for the stars involved, but great news for Philly. In the show's second week the bus screeched to a halt outside the Prince Music Theater, where a hometown audience, with good taste and pop smarts, would elect their favourite act in this great fame experiment. The stars on the stage were shining, big cutout stars posed at freewheeling angles with light attractively pouring through from backstage. From under one branch peeps Davina McCall, pixie-esque presenter, inescapable on British TV, who helpfully introduces herself, taking her new found anonymity in her stride.

'As preamble she helps us get the hang of clapping

for TV, that is, much louder and harder than feels natural or deserved. We sit very still while she tapes five-second trailers for the following evening's airing, hyping the eviction of the loser, one of the two least popular in New Orleans, who is then knocked out by British viewers. "Who's going home, Sonia or Dollar?" she utters mysteriously to camera two. Once that's in the can, we see the first performer.

'Gina G, one-hit wonder and UK veteran of Eurovision Song Contest 1996, steps out on to the stage. She's wearing a window treatment designed for a very small window. Nervous, she's the first to perform from the mandated Philly Sound roster, choosing Gamble & Huff's "Don't Leave Me This Way" but eschews the original style in favour of the 1986 full-disco-glory version by The Communards, synths and all. It's all very wrong. Our giggles are shown, no doubt, to the viewers at home. We're doing well with the clapping, we're told – particularly Luke. Luke is four and in the ninth row with his dad. Davina thinks he's "ace". She also thinks Philly's brilliant. "My little daughter and I found this amazing museum yesterday – with little shopping carts. What's it called? The Touch-Me Museum?" We correct her.

'Haydon Eshun used to be a child star: aged nine, he rapped at the front of boy band Ultimate Kaos. Now 20, hot and ripe for a comeback, he proceeds to kick "I'll Make Love To You", doing his best better-than-Boyz II Men impression. To schoolgirl cheers, he dashes offstage, then reappears, blushing, to retrieve the shirt he'd shed mid-performance. Not all the eight performers tonight are complete unknowns. Peter Cox used to sing with Go West, whose biggest hit, "King of Wishful Thinking", at least made it into *Pretty Woman*; and, when Tony Hadley, lead singer of eighties new romantics Spandau Ballet steps out, Davina hums the chorus of "Gold", so we're all up to speed.

'Who's left? Michelle Gayle, ex-*EastEnders* actress turned nineties pop princess, comes out looking gorgeous and hardly flustered. She sails soulfully through "The Whole Town's Laughing at Me". There was, politely, no laughter when Elkie Brooks, a songstress with a 20-year successful career, suffered the night's worst treatment. Without the glitz of recognition, she was received as if she was someone's tipsy aunt.

'As the showdown looms, we finally meet eighties disco outfit Dollar and Liverpudlian bubbly songbird Sonia, both up for eviction and apparently punch-buddies, starting fights on the bus. Mitigating circumstances: performers must slum it early on, working their way up, no Four Seasons for them. Their experience of Philly was of no running water.

Sonia, now sadly slimmed down from "bubbly" to "sylph-like", grins forcibly the entire time before shaking with relief as last episode's viewer verdict is announced. She stays. Dollar leaves without performing for us.

'Now, we're instructed to vote. Precisely half of us have keypads, so in electoral spirit, the rest of us indulge in voter intimidation. While buttons are pressed, Davina tapes a competition segment: A weekend trip to Philly for anyone who knows who starred in *Philadelphia*: Tom Cruise or Tom Hanks? "*Den-zel*," shouts one girl, whose neighbour shakes her placard (Liberty Bell hearts UK) vigorously. The votes are in. Peter Cox wins by a nose while Gina and Elkie must face the text-message votes of the harsh British public for possible eviction. Somewhere the flickering flame of fame democracy gutters. But we clap all the same, TV-style.'

Two years after Davina's show, and with perhaps an entirely different, slightly less challenging approach, *Hit Me Baby One More Time* hosted by Vernon Kay used a similar concept. It offered rebirth to pop stars who had been out of the limelight for years with the opportunity to prove their worth on national television and have a second shot at regaining their lost fame and fortune. It certainly made a change to the – by then – old and tired formula of searching for someone who could be turned into another Will Young or Gareth Gates since their successes on what now seemed like a countless round of reality talent shows.

And, if any proof were needed that it could work, then Shakin' Stevens proved it when he won the show in the spring of 2005 and found himself swiftly returned to the spotlight in Britain. The format of the show was that during each programme five former pop stars would sing their biggest hit, along with a cover version of a contemporary hit. Each week one winner was picked from each show by a phone vote leading to the grand final when the overall winner could release a single featuring both songs. For Stevens the show worked a treat. Not only did it place him back in the singles charts for the first time since 1992, it also propelled him back into promoting a new hits compilation and taking off on a UK concert tour. Even if it was, as some reckoned, the last brick in a carefully constructed campaign to relaunch his career, it worked.

But if the critics or even the public weren't that keen on *Reborn In The USA*, what did they think about *Popstars: The Rivals*, which Davina had presented six months before *Reborn*? It was the sequel to *Pop Stars*, the series that spawned chart-topping band Hear'say and pop idols Will Young, Gareth Gates and Darius.

Like its predecessor, it was the sort of programme where possible stars of the future could be discovered and put on the road to fame. Or it could be where the dreams of the young hopefuls fighting for a place in an all too often brutal treatment of desperation for fame would be completely dashed forever. For *Rivals*, the idea was, as the show's title suggested, to create a girl and boy band that could battle it out for the Christmas number one. By the time the third programme was aired on 21 September, 112 hopefuls had all been called back. Over half of them would soon be reduced to tears as they were whittled down to a mere 50 by judges Geri Halliwell, Pete Waterman and Louis Walsh, fighting between themselves to produce the winning band.

Not all the applicants were heartbroken at not getting placed, however. One girl was just satisfied to have made it to the second round and even posted a message on an internet forum under her online name of *londongirl*. 'Woo, today I went down to the *Popstars* auditions with some friends for a laugh and I met Davina McCall, who was just soooooooooo lovely and funny, and Pete Waterman, who was his usual cheesy self. Unfortunately I didn't get to meet Geri Halliwell (maybe that's a good thing) because I didn't get through to the second stage because they thought I was more of a solo artist. Pah! Still, it was sooo fun and I got to meet so many people and the atmosphere was excellent. I even got on the news – WAHAY! There were all these photographers and journalists, it was mad. Some people there were taking it so seriously as if their life depended on it!'

Assistant producer Barnaby Coughlin, who had also worked with Davina on *Big Brother*, would probably agree. He explained that it was during the filming process of these hopefuls that some of the most nerve-racking moments were produced. 'First they sang as a group, then one by one in front of each other. It's been completely mad. *Big Brother* was an epic experience and this is another big reality-TV juggernaut where you're thrown in at the deep end and end up auditioning kids from all over the country.'

It was he continued, a very testing time for all, but it was also thoroughly enjoyable. 'It's great to see the kids emerge. They come on with their mums, open their mouths, have amazing voices and you can see how they can be nurtured. The little 16-year-olds have all done so well. They're staying in the same hotel, so there's incredible bonding going on between them. We've had amazing attitudes. Hazel from Ireland, for instance, is a 22-year-old who is eight months' pregnant and has an amazing voice. A 23-year-old magician called Daniel also had a fantastic voice and look.' Certainly, 'the look of a star can be as important as their voice. But, when it came to nerves, Geri persuaded everyone to start screaming. Geri has been fantastic. She works the kids well, as, coming from their camp, she's experienced what they have. She got them doing primal screaming, which is very LA, which got all their energy levels up. She knows what she wants, and Pete knows what he wants, and what his band is going to be.'

It was during the October and November shows that the finalists took to the stage every Saturday night, singing for their place in one of the two bands. One contestant was eliminated each week until the final line-ups emerged. The resulting female line-up became Girls Aloud, to be managed by Louis Walsh. And the winning boy band was called One True Voice and fell under the guidance of Pete Waterman. Although in the end the boy band didn't live up to the expectation that they would be more successful than the girls, and almost confirming the pitfalls of being primed for instant stardom in the way that they were, they disbanded after just two singles. Girls Aloud, however, remain successful to this day, and although One True Voice are no longer together, they did give the girls a good run for their money in the battle for the symbolic Christmas number one. But the girls won hands down when their single, 'Sound of the Underground', stayed in the top slot for four weeks.

Although Davina's role was presenter, host and link between contestants and judges, there were moments when it also became quite fraught. Like the time on the first show in November when she announced that Chloe had been voted out of the running and a member of the studio audience ranted abuse about how the vote was daylight robbery, it was a fix, and was complete and utter rubbish. It was perhaps one of the few times when television audiences would witness Davina being totally stunned by such an unexpected outburst. All she could do was look on in stony silence.

She was not quite so stunned, but completely thrilled, four months earlier when she was awarded the Millennium Volunteers highest accolade for her work with charity and voluntary organisations. In fact, she was only the second person to have ever received an Honorary MV (Millennium Volunteer) by young people inspired by her commitment to volunteering. The only other person to have received the same accolade, the previous year, was Prince William for his voluntary work in Chile. Interestingly enough, Davina's award coincided with the publication of a new report demonstrating the success of MV, particularly in its significant contribution to communities and its positive affect on volunteers' lives. Davina, of course, was absolutely delighted to be given the award. 'It's been a joy being the patron of

FOCUS. As it's such a small charity, all the fundraising we've done has made such a big difference. Thanks to MV for this recognition – I'll make sure I keep it up.'

Stephen Twigg MP, then Minister for Young People and Learning, who headed the Millennium Volunteers programme, could not have been happier. 'I'm pleased that the Millennium Volunteer National Youth Forum wants to give this award to Davina. By volunteering so much of her time to projects such as the charity group FOCUS and "Make a Difference Day", as well as her support for the World Wildlife Fund and people with AIDS in Uganda, she has shown how even very busy people can make a difference. Volunteering not only helps others, but also gives young people life experiences not easily gained at school or college. Millennium Volunteers provides young people with inspiring opportunities relevant to their own personal passions and interests, encouraging them to channel their energies positively while playing an active role in their local communities.'

Certainly, that is what the then latest research confirmed. It showed that volunteers were carrying out crucial local work, such as setting up youth and drug projects, tackling racism, helping younger children with reading, conservation and a range of cultural activities. And the new figures, only just collected at the time of Davina's award, showed that there were nearly 65,000 MV volunteers nationwide, almost half of which had never considered volunteering before. Even better was the fact that over 24,000 volunteers had received their 100-hour certificates and nearly 16,000 volunteers had successfully completed their 200-hours Award of Excellence. Even then, this trend indicated that the Millennium Volunteers programme was well on track to meet the target of 100,000 volunteers by December 2003. Amid fierce competition, Davina had been selected for the award after an overwhelming vote by the Millennium Volunteers National Youth Forum.

Reena Patel, Chairperson of the National Youth Forum, also agreed with Twigg: 'The National Youth Forum represents over 65,000 young people, who are gaining valuable experience and making a difference to their local communities through Millennium Volunteers. In an overwhelming vote, the Youth Forum chose Davina McCall as the recipient of the next Honorary MV for her outstanding work with voluntary and charity organisations. We hope that, by highlighting the inspiring efforts of people in the public eye, it will in turn encourage other young people who would not have considered volunteering before to get involved.'

And, if any further proof were needed of Davina's

commitment to charity, Steve Corlett remembers the time when, as he puts it, 'It was the biggest night in my advertising career – hosting a reception to launch the NSPCC's new TV campaign that hopes to end cruelty to children forever. Phew! They were all there, the good, the wealthy and the not as famous as they'd like to be. The list of celebs was up to a massive four. There was Richard Dunwoody, Dermot O'Leary, Noel Edmonds. But there was still someone missing – the grand hostess of the night. Then, in a flash of cameras and gasps, she strode through the doors: Davina McCall. My hands started to sweat, my heart skipped a beat. I knew that I was supposed to brief her on the commercials we were showing. She was led into a meeting room where I had set up some light refreshments for her, and I made my way over. I walked into the room and introduced myself; she did the same. My faltering voice perhaps betrayed my nervousness, but I think I got away with it.

'After a few pleasantries about the journey, her job and her new baby Holly – very beautiful, she showed me a picture – her assistant asked me to put on the tapes of the ads. I played the commercials and at the end turned around to speak to Davina. I looked at her and noticed her eyes were welling up; a couple of tears formed on her perfectly treated eyelashes and dropped softly on to her face. She then said, "Wonderful… brilliant… they are so powerful and moving."

'"Yes," I said, "we wanted to shake people out of the comfort zone and make them take responsibility for stopping child abuse."

'"Well, you've certainly done that," Davina replied.

'I then said, "Well, I'll let you look through your speech. See you later."

'"Bye," she said.

'Ahh, Davina McCall – my new best friend and comrade in keeping our children free from cruelty… Oh, and I made her cry.'

11

REALITY BITES

In the summer of 2004, Davina was worried sick. Although it seemed as if she had never been off our screens, she was concerned that she was about to make a mess of her so-called comeback after a seven-month hiatus of maternity absence, even though she hadn't really been away. But it wasn't as if she was a resurgent pop star, launching herself in one last desperate attempt to grab the national limelight. So why was she so worried? She was concerned simply because, like anyone who takes a long break, she was finding the fearful prospect of returning to work a bit daunting. And it probably didn't help matters that she had already stopped thinking of herself as Davina the TV presenter and was feeling 'more like Davina, the milk factory' from all the breast feeding. As she said, it was just 'scary coming back to it'.

In the time that she had been away from the screen and the limelight, it appeared, as one journalist remarked, that she had gone 'potty about being in labour'. Just nine months after the arrival of her second daughter, she listed giving birth as her favourite thing. Giving birth, she said, is 'absolutely at the top of my list. I love it to the point of being evangelical. It's by far the best and most incredible experience of my life. Everyone thinks I was really brave, but I wasn't. And every time I meet a pregnant woman, I want to remind her to enjoy the experience. Don't get me wrong, it does hurt but it is different to other pain.'

So enthralled was she with it all that she was already thinking about how she would like to have another child if only she could talk her husband Matthew round to it. 'I can't bear the idea of saying I won't have any more children but I'd have a lot of persuading to do with Matthew. Maybe, if I told him it would be a boy, he might be up for it. But I think he wants his wife back.' Perhaps it was because Davina had been raised by her grandparents after the breakdown of her own parents' marriage that motherhood was now making her think differently about her own childhood. 'It makes you very grateful to anyone who parented you because it is such a hard job. I say thank you to my parents and my granny endlessly.' Not only that, she continued but, 'motherhood has made me feel a whole person. There was a little part of me before that needed to be filled. Having Holly and Tilly has made me feel complete. But I do think I've become less driven.'

That being 'less driven', as she calls it, was all to do with her ambition to succeed in her career. 'When I first started out in TV, I worked six days a week and I don't want to do that any more. My life is about seeking balance and now I've found that. Having the first baby was such a shock to the system because Matthew and I were so selfish before, going off and doing whatever we wanted, when we wanted. Then, all of a sudden, there's a baby and you can't do that. The second time around you don't miss the lost spontaneity so it's all fine.' Although her happiness at home was now matched by the success she had worked so hard to achieve on the small screen, she still insisted that motherhood had encouraged her to cut back on what once seemed like a never-ending round of hectic filming schedules and appearances. 'It made me want to redress my work–life balance – I try to work less than I did before I had Holly.'

The couple's second daughter Tilly was born on 23 September 2003, exactly one day after first daughter

Holly's second birthday. She was a 'huge' baby, laughed Davina. 'She was 9lb 11oz. Bonny for her, but not so bonny for me.' And adding to the joy of it all, Davina repeated, was her lifelong wish to be surrounded by lots of kids and a Noah's Ark of pets – 'I want ponies, pot-bellied pigs, donkeys and swings – and children tugging on my apron strings as I cook.' Once again, Davina couldn't shower enough praise on her 'amazing' midwives, this time, Pam and Jenny. And now she had two children, there was obviously a question as to whether or not she would employ a nanny, like most other celebrities. No, she didn't think she would, because one of the things she enjoyed most was walking round the house naked. Certainly, there is a nice freedom in being able to do that in the privacy of your own home, or even hanging out in a dressing gown for a whole day. So it is perhaps easy to understand why she wouldn't want anyone else roaming around. As Davina pointed out, they were more than happy with their clan of Robertsons, just the way they were.

Although it took a five-hour labour for Tilly to be delivered, perhaps that was because this time she opted for a water birth. She had tried the same thing with Holly, 'but everything slowed down too much when I got in the water so they made me get out and walk up and down the stairs. It was barbaric. But both births were good – I mean they were long and very painful – but, when I look back at it, it was a really positive, empowering, spiritual thing to go through. And I also think that doing it drug-free, even though it's a lot more painful, gives you a sense of pride at the end.'

Perhaps it was because she considered the experience so uplifting that she was planning to make a documentary to look at why women aren't getting all the information they need when it comes to having a baby. 'I don't understand why the only place a woman can safely labour in a maternity unit is on the bed,' she says, quickly warming to her subject. 'The worst position for a woman to be in labour is on her back. I went down the normal obstetric route for the first 20 weeks of my first pregnancy, but the more I talked to my obstetrician, the more I realised I wasn't on the same wavelength as him. It was a girlfriend who'd had two home births that brought me round to the idea of them.'

Since the birth of Tilly, she found motherhood had been a lot easier. 'Everybody's different, but I've found it easier this time because I'm a bit more confident. I know what I'm doing and I'm less stressed about it all – I'm not getting much sleep, though.' Although she had obviously taken time off work to give birth to Tilly, there was another reason why she wanted to remain more elusive than she had in the past. She felt she needed to give herself a break from what she says seemed like an almost endless run of presenting jobs that had taken up most of the previous 12 months prior to her maternity leave. After *Popstars: The Rivals*, she went on to present the *Brit Awards*, *Big Brother* and *Reborn In The USA*. She was the first to admit that it was perhaps a little too much. 'It's funny because everyone's been saying it was manic for me in 2003 but I actually stopped work in August. But it's been quite good to have the time off because I think people were sick to death of me.'

Certainly, she would be treading much more carefully so as not to repeat the over exposure she felt preceded Tilly's arrival in the world. And she was now more determined than ever that viewers wouldn't be seeing as much of her as they had before. After *Love On A Saturday Night*, and once again sneaking around outside the *Big Brother* house and giving big hugs to the evicted house mates in a fifth series of the show, she was again promising herself some time away from work. On top of her television commitments, she was also on a military-style health and fitness regime that she had been putting herself through ever since she was five months' pregnant. 'It's brilliant. But I've trained so hard – I had to work like a squaddie.' And that was certainly true of the way she got into shape after the birth of Tilly. On the advice of friends, she had gone to ex-Marines officer Mark Wren. He put her on his 3 Scheme plan, so-called because she would exercise three times a week on three different types of training and would eat three meals a day when perhaps she didn't before.

Not so good, for Davina, was the limit of three treats per week, like chocolate or a cream cake. But there wasn't any specific diet. As before, without her health regime, she would allow herself the normal portions of fruit, vegetables, protein, fat and carbohydrates. The only ruling was that there could not be any carbohydrates in her evening meal and snacks between meals were strictly banned. 'When I'm pregnant, I eat enough for 10 but I have to stay svelte because I work in television. It's really dire looking at yourself and thinking, "I've got to get fit again." I've lost a stone and a half, but it's not just a case of ditching the cream buns – I eat sensibly and exercise.'

To get to the svelte condition that Davina wanted to achieve, she was working out with Mark and his wife Jackie three times a week at their Off The Mark Fitness Gym in Surrey. She would pump iron and tackle kickboxing, karate, boxing, swimming, cycling, distance running, cross training and sprints. The training was pretty intense and she would burn at least 800 calories per session. A former gymnast,

Jackie couldn't have been more proud of Davina. 'She always puts in 110 per cent effort – the results are all down to her hard work. No two training sessions were the same. Davina does a very varied training programme. I may do body sculpting, toning and stretching in one session, and Mark will do boxing, rowing and weights the next. We mix it in threes.' And Mark and Jackie also encouraged a healthy eating plan with three balanced meals a day.

Davina was thrilled with the results. 'I feel much better about myself when I'm slimmer. Two days ago I managed to fit into my pre-pregnancy black trousers. I'm very pleased about that.' Not that she would be content with just returning to her pre-pregnancy weight of 10 stone. She was going to make sure she would drop her weight down even further than that. You can imagine how good she must have felt when she weighed herself and found out she weighed just nine stone. As she says, it was all down to her workouts, which she describes as good old-fashioned hard work, and, even though some have accused her of going too far, she was delighted with her new look. 'I feel much better about myself when I'm slimmer. I definitely feel sexier, too. I'm realistic, though. I'm a 37-year-old mother of two. I'm never going to have Cat Deeley's legs or Kylie's bum; I'm never going to be a skinny-minny, but I don't mind that. My husband loves my bottom – and that is what's important. When I look in the mirror now, I see a slimmer, more toned version of what I do have, and that's OK. I haven't dieted or detoxed, there are no fads.

'I put on so much weight when I get pregnant,' she continued. 'And, of course, I'm in denial that it has anything to do with the enormous amounts of pudding I eat. I always pay at the end of it, and it has got to go some time. And I definitely feel the pressure to stay slim – I am self-critical. After I had Tilly, I put on a lot of weight and when I started bits and bobs on telly I found it hard to look at myself. It is difficult being in the public eye and changing shape – you feel like you are on show most of the time. I have to stay svelte because I work in TV. I'm not somebody who naturally twangs back into shape; there's no quick-fix solution and there's no magic wand you can wave. I have to put in the hard graft, and start exercising and eating sensibly.'

In the end it was worth it, and 'I love Jackie and Mark for making me feel semi-good about my body again. I blew up to the size of a small country when I was expecting but that's because I ate whatever I wanted. It's been hard to shift the weight but it looks much better if you're toned. You look after your body, you look after your mind.' With that kind of inspirational talk, it was hardly surprising that, when over 1,000 women were asked to choose a celebrity as their ideal running buddy in a survey by Cancer Research UK's *Race For Life*, it was Davina whose name came out on top.

By the time she went to the Caribbean on her family holiday, when Tilly was just four months old, her determination to get slim again certainly looked like it had paid off. It was also evident from the paparazzi pictures that appeared in almost every tabloid just what a big kid at heart she could be, splashing around with a plastic bucket, wading into the warm waters and chatting with fellow holidaymakers on the beach. And, like the proud mother she was, showing off her new daughter to pop star Sonique, who was staying at the same exclusive resort.

It was probably where the story that Davina had apparently told a journalist came from. 'A man came up to me recently and said, "It must be difficult going out with such a handsome man." I told him that it wasn't, because I had two things that other girls haven't got. He thought I was talking about my boobs! I was like, "Nooo, not my boobs, our children!" I am the mother of Matthew's children and nothing or nobody can take that away.' Perhaps her ingredient for a happy marriage was how she and Matthew laugh a lot, which she considered really important. 'We are like every couple: all relationships go through ups and downs but it's worth riding it out. Everybody needs love in their life, and Matthew really is so lovely – I can't believe how lucky I have been.'

When she returned from holiday, she started *Love On A Saturday Night*, which was, according to some, essentially ITV1's replacement for Cilla Black's *Blind Date*. But was it? The upside to the show, as far as Davina was concerned, and fitting in with her criterion to work less, was the fact that she would only be required three days a week for filming. Although *Blind Date* had been one of the most popular of all dating shows on primetime television since it was launched in 1985, 18 years later its audience had plummeted. Drastic changes to the show just made it look even more dire than it was, so perhaps it shouldn't have been surprising when, at the beginning of Cilla's 40th anniversary on television, she calmly decided to walk out. It happened during a live edition of the show. Cilla did her normal piece to the camera and then stunned the whole of the UK, including her own bosses, by announcing it was her last series. Then she calmly walked off camera and out of the studio.

If she wanted a dramatic exit, she certainly got it, but, as Davina made clear to all those who asked, *Love On A Saturday Night* wasn't trying to be *Blind Date*. Nor would it be attempting to replace it. If anything, *Love* would have its own format and be as far removed from *Blind Date* as possible. That's why the programme would have Davina and sidekick Jonathan Wilkes springing surprises on members of the public as they attempted to fix them up with dates live on TV. Even though from the same tradition as *Oblivious*, it was probably slightly better. One of the things that made it better would be the match-making games designed to bring men and women together.

Still a true romantic at heart, it was the ideal show for Davina. This is most evident from each series of *Big Brother* when she spends the entire time willing the housemates to turn their flirting into a full-blown romance while the majority of viewers wonder if they're going to have sex on national television. Yes, she agrees, 'I'm obsessed with dating and I'm renowned for trying to match-make. I've had a couple of successes where sparks have flown so now it will be great to have the chance to fix some more people up on TV. You never know what could happen.'

In one show, *Love On A Saturday Night* would feature one single girl dating three boys at once, all of them in masks, while, in another, desperate and dateless viewers would be given a makeover by experts. And, in a bid to make the show suitable for all the family, an elderly Mrs Merton-style couple would be treated to some modern approaches to romance, such as speed dating. The idea of the show, reflected one executive at Granada Television, the network responsible for production, was to make it 'good, clean fun with the added spice of being live where anything can happen, and Davina is a natural for the show. There's just nobody better than her at keeping together a live broadcast.'

Asked to describe the format of the show, Davina told journalists that it would incorporate a very loose format in which she and co-presenter Wilkes would try various methods to find dates for lovelorn contestants. 'Jonathan will broadcast from somewhere round the country where he'll be doing makeovers, and I'll be surprising audience members and helping kids choose partners for their mum or dad who's hopeless at dating. There's also a 'second chance at love' bit where somebody gets to meet up with three of their exes, who all want to get back with them, and they can choose which one they want to go out for dinner with.'

Perhaps more than any other, Davina was in her element with such a show, as it offered her free rein to do with complete strangers what she already does with her mates: sort out their love lives – 'I am chronic when it comes to matchmaking. It's got to the point now where I'm just really annoying. But I've got one on the go at the moment. My friend got so used to me trying to match-make him he just gave in and took a girl's number off me and they're going out next week.' And, if that wasn't enough, she continues, 'I drive all my mates nuts constantly setting them up on blind dates, but to be perfectly honest I haven't had a wedding yet. But I live in hope and maybe I'll get lucky on the show. So to be able to match-make every Saturday night is a dream come true – I'll have to get some of my single friends on the show, starting with Rachel, 24, gorgeous, enjoys outdoor pursuits – and indoor ones! She would make a wonderful girlfriend.'

12

SEX, LIES &
BIG BROTHER

Five months into 2005, it was obvious that Davina was much more at ease with her physical appearance than ever before. That was when she stripped down to a bikini on national television to interview *Big Brother* evictee and pathological undresser Sam Heuston, who would exit the house on the 22nd day of the sixth series. Not only was Sam a serial undresser, she was also bisexual and had almost constantly worn her bikini since entering the house three weeks previously. Towards the end of the interview, with Davina in her bikini, the audience were going so wild that Davina more or less gave up with her questions and, using Sam's favourite motto, simply said, 'Let's just kiss.' Before Sam knew what was happening, Davina had planted a smacker on her lips. Good kisser or not, it probably reminded Sam of her snog with housemate Makosi Musambasi earlier that same week. Despite the booing crowd and one onlooker even hurling a drink over her, sex-mad Sam confessed that she loved Makosi, and considered her the best snogger in the house.

The idea for the bikini, Davina remembers, 'was just a funny idea I had in the production meeting. So we got three or four bikinis and I tried them on to see what I looked like sitting down, to make sure there was no overhang. I thought, "I feel comfortable with this because I'll be sitting down with my cards in front of me," but I forgot that I had to get up and walk to the front of the stage, and the audience was behind me. I am happy with my body, but that is above and beyond. Their heads were up my bum! But it was weirdly liberating. I only did it because it made us laugh. It doesn't mean I'm trying to become a sex goddess – I'm not like that at all; I'm not a pin-up.'

Besides, she continued, 'I like doing naughty things that people don't expect of me and sometimes that gets me into trouble – like, whenever I see any paparazzi, for some reason I want to flash! But I've grown out of that. I must do it because I'm nearly 40, I've had two children and my boobs [now without pierced nipples] aren't what they used to be.' All the same there were still some who considered her a pin-up. Friend and confidante Jackie Clune's brother was one of them. According to Clune, not only is he obsessed with her, but also considers her the ideal woman. It is probably true to say that Davina McCall is not only seen as one of the boys, but she is also a big hit with them.

Whether or not she enjoys being thought of as a pin-up, it was during this series of *Big Brother* that she would come in for some sharp criticism about her treatment of Makosi when she was evicted from the house on Day 78. In fact, Makosi, and indeed *Big Brother* itself, became the subject of something far more controversial than just her interview with Davina. In a story that appeared in the *Sun* during the final week of the series, it was claimed that a talent agency had invoiced the producers of *Big Brother* for £609 for procuring Makosi's services. And, on top of that, in the same story it was also alleged that this proved that she was in fact an actress rather than a genuine contestant. Although the claim was denied by *Big Brother* with the explanation that the money was paid to the talent agency (which did not represent Makosi) for work relating to the supplementary show *Big Brother's Big Mouth.*

Interestingly enough, and despite Makosi's eventual unpopularity, she was one of the favourites to win the show in the first five weeks. On week two, when all the housemates were up for eviction, Makosi received the least amount of public votes to evict. However, in week six, she shocked the nation by allegedly having sex in the pool with Anthony and later revealing that she thought she might be pregnant. At one point a tearful Makosi asked *Big Brother* for a pregnancy test and contemplated that she would name the child Jacuzzi. Anthony strongly and repeatedly denied they had full intercourse.

In the end, she came third with 8.9% of the vote, but her interview with Davina was poorly received, with the audience booing and shouting 'liar' at Makosi all the way through. As the interview neared its end, chants of 'off, off, off!' were yelled by the crowd. Four hundred and fifty viewers complained to Channel 4 about both the interview and Davina's unusually harsh manner. Makosi herself has since admitted that she found the interview 'distressing' and that she felt Davina did nothing to support her when the crowd heckled her. Soon after leaving the house, Makosi spoke of her ill mother, her regret at 'having unprotected sex' with Anthony in the pool and admitted it was a bad example to youth, especially as she was a nurse and should have known better.

Despite her professed regret, she still attended an Edinburgh festival entitled *I Had Sex On TV* to give a discussion on safe sex.

After the series ended, the *Sun* did another piece to reveal that Makosi's former lover from before her appearance on *Big Brother*, and with whom she had had unprotected sex, was HIV positive. Fearing that she might have contracted the disease, Makosi had herself tested: the result was negative. Three months after *Big Brother 6* ended that August, the immigration services curtailed her visa as she had left her job as a cardiac nurse to appear on *Big Brother*. Makosi appealed the ruling, claiming she faced death if she returned to Zimbabwe. In November 2005, she retained the right to stay in the UK.

As for Davina's interview, was it really that bad? According to the press, yes, it was. In fact, it was reported that 'the *Big Brother* bosses received 450 complaints over Davina's eviction interview with Makosi. She showed little sympathy for Makosi as the crowd outside the *Big Brother* house booed and heckled her. Makosi said she was disgusted that the presenter did not support her when hostile onlookers screamed "liar, liar!" Instead of calming the baying crowd, Davina told Makosi, "I can't believe you're showing no remorse." Part of the problem seemed to be that Makosi had been accused of lying about having sex with winner Anthony Hutton. Even the official *Big Brother* online fan site blamed Davina for failing to control the crowd. A spokesman for TV regulator Ofcom confirmed they would be looking into the complaints.'

Elsewhere, it was much the same story. In some quarters, it was Davina's attitude that was said to be at the root of the problem. 'Despite Makosi's insistence that she was upset and distressed by the abusive crowd, Davina continued the interview regardless.' According to a number of web forums on the internet, most were urging viewers to make a complaint to Ofcom about how Makosi was treated. One post at Digital Spy read, 'I have just finished watching Channel 4's *Big Brother* and I am ashamed and disgusted by the [lack of] impartiality shown by the presenter Davina McCall to one of the contestants: Makosi. I felt she was very unprofessional and let her personal feelings for Makosi get in the way of her job. Davina is supposed to be presenting the programme, not being a moral judge! I'm also at a loss to the lack of consistency in her interviewing technique. For instance, Craig was clearly booed by the crowd but was soothed by Davina in his interview. Why wasn't the same treatment afforded to Makosi? Why didn't Davina intervene to quieten the crowd? These are just a few of the incidences that clearly showed Davina's bias. I would please like a reply from you as I have been very disturbed by this event.'

And another wrote, 'Love her or loathe her, Makosi was one of the most entertaining people in the *Big Brother* house this year. From her "secret task" on the very first night, the romp with Anthony in the pool, the "pregnancy scare" to referring to herself constantly as Makosi, she (and possibly Derek) kept the show interesting. It's funny how the viewers forget that *BB* is a television programme and a competition. Isn't it surprising that people will vote for dull-as-dishwater Anthony and not for someone as colourful as Makosi?'

There were, however, a few who spoke up in Davina's defence. When asked on another internet forum if Davina had been unfair, no 'I don't think so,' said Brad Mullett. 'Makosi proved that she is a game player during her time in the *Big Brother* house. She was shrewd in her dealings with folk and not shy about speaking her mind. Davina knows that the *Big Brother* contestants are in the competition for fame and fortune, and this year's *Big Brother* is no exception. While Makosi would have faced a tough time on the night, it would only have lasted a few hours then she'd be weighing up her options for interviews, TV shows, etc. Yes, Davina could probably have done a bit more to settle the crowd, but it all added to the drama of the experience – compare it to Anthony's brief-but-dull interview.'

Not only was Davina's interview up for criticism, but also the entire series of *Big Brother* for operating at what was described as 'the limits of acceptability' by the broadcasting watchdog Ofcom. In their ruling, they were concerned over the scenes in which Makosi and Anthony appeared to have sex in the pool and Kinga simulated sex with a wine bottle and, although both 'did amount to potentially dangerous behaviour', it was unlikely to have led to copycat behaviour. Channel 4 admitted the incident was 'shocking' but said they were obliged to give a true picture of events in the house. Davina was cleared of racial discrimination over her so-called hostile interview with Makosi.

By the time the furore of *Big Brother 6* had died down and a new *Celebrity Big Brother* was already under way on Channel 4 with the likes of Bez, Brigitte Nielsen, Caprice, Jackie Stallone and Germaine Greer, Davina had launched a new Saturday-evening primetime show on BBC1. Coincidentally, this was the first she had fronted for the channel that would, in a few months' time, announce plans for Davina to become their first female primetime chat-show host.

He's Having A Baby was, to all intents and purposes, a parenting show that featured eight young men on their very different journeys to becoming first-time dads, all struggling to cope with the dramatic, funny and difficult changes parenthood brings. The due dates of their children are staggered throughout the run of the show. Over 10 weeks from late August, *He's Having a Baby* captured the lives of these men as they prepared to take on perhaps the greatest challenge that life presents – the birth of their first child – providing a unique insight into the pressures faced by modern British fathers.

To help them prepare for fatherhood, the dads-to-be were all put through a series of 'Dad Assignments' that gave them first-hand experience of just what lay ahead. Grabbing them by the scruff of the neck and throwing them into a variety of situations with children of all ages, they would be getting 18 years' worth of parenting crammed into just 10 hectic, hilarious, non-stop weeks. How they coped as they were tormented by tiny tots and teenage tearaways was what the BBC hoped would attract the viewers. Davina's role in the show was to interview the eight men every Saturday evening live in the studio so that she could question each of them about their unique and compelling stories from the previous week.

Viewers could also keep up to date throughout the week with the progress each father-to-be was making on a nightly BBC3 programme capturing their daily lives in real-life soap-opera style, showing how they were coping with the ever-changing emotions and demands of becoming a parent for the first time. There would also be a chance to see how the dads were getting on in the eyes of close friends and family – and, of course, the mums-to-be. Were their partners going into fatherhood with their eyes wide open, or were they better suited to sitting in the pub talking about football than talking about their feelings?

For Davina, it seemed like the perfect vehicle for her debut on a new channel. 'I really can't wait to do this programme. It's a well-known fact I'm evangelical about birth. I'm really looking forward to helping prepare these dads for the best journey of their lives. Men largely get ignored when it comes to pregnancy, birth and becoming a parent, so it's time to give them a helping hand.'

Leon Wilde, Hat Trick's head of entertainment, the production company behind the programme, agreed: 'This isn't a how-to-parent show – we're not trying to tell people how to be a dad, but are saying that it's cool to be a dad.'

One of the first-time fathers was Jason Pennycooke, a 32-year-old actor and choreographer, who lived with his 25-year-old partner Debbie in North London. The couple met three years before they were picked for the show while they were playing the romantic leads in the West End musical *Rent*. They were expecting their first child that October and Jason was relishing the prospect. 'I think I will make a fantastic dad because I am a child at heart. It is something that I've always wanted to do. I came from a broken home, so it's quite nice for my child to have something that I didn't have.' And certainly Davina's co-presenter, comedian Danny Wallace, reckoned that Jason would be fine, if none of the assignments involved nappy changing. 'That's the one thing I'm a bit nervous about,' said Jason. 'But this series is a fantastic way to document your child's arrival into this world.' Although Jason and Debbie had agreed on a name if it was a girl, Jason was secretly hoping for a little boy. 'Everyone thinks it's going to be a boy, and it would be nice because, if we have a little girl later, then he can look after her.'

Like many expectant fathers, Jason's excitement was tempered by a few fears. 'The main thing I'm nervous about – as any new father would be – is the responsibility. I keep thinking, "Will I be a good dad and am I going to be able to stay in work long enough to provide for my young family?" But hopefully that won't be a problem.' At the time Jason was back in the West End performing in *The Big Life*, the first ever black British musical. He would also have to learn about getting the right balance in his home and work life – and what about his social life? 'It'll have to go on a bit of a backburner for a while, but otherwise having a child should slot in quite easy, I hope.' Jason and Debbie's daughter, Saffron Jay Pennycooke, was born on 30 September 2005.

But, after just two weeks, the show was moved to the earlier 5.30 teatime slot and cut from a ten-week to an eight-week run in an effort to save it from being axed altogether. The show apparently lost 600,000 viewers on its launch weekend to its ITV1 rival *The X-Factor*, which pulled in 7.2 million viewers with a peak of 8.2 million. The talent contest, starring Simon Cowell, Sharon Osbourne and Louis Walsh, was up 600,000 viewers on the previous week. Peter Fincham, who had taken over control of the Beeb three months previously, told guests at the Edinburgh International TV Festival, 'In entertainment there's a big and never-ending challenge. Entertainment needs to be at the core of BBC1. It's also one of the hardest and most challenging genres to succeed in. We felt the show was right for Saturday night – it has a different flavour to the *X-Factor*, and Davina is a great talent and it's brilliant to have her on BBC1.'

All the same, it was a huge disappointment, especially to Davina, who, as one would expect, had 'put her all into the show and having the series pulled two weeks early was very upsetting'.

According to the *Mirror*, a spokesperson for the programme said, 'There is always some risk involved in producing experimental shows and we are very proud of the results. It's felt the show can explore all it set out at the start in its now reduced eight-week run.'

Despite the criticism, Davina still spoke out against the critics who had slammed the show as a non-starter. Perhaps one of the problems was the fact that the opening show didn't really focus on an everyday typical working couple. After all, Jason and Debbie were to all intents and purposes in showbiz. All the same, Davina stood by the comments she made to Britain's *Heat* magazine that she was 100 per cent behind the show, no matter what, saying, 'If anybody hasn't watched it – which I think is quite a lot of you – you should give it a go, because it's a very good show.' And she blamed poor viewing figures on the success of *The X-Factor*, which launched on the same night; no one had foreseen that *He's Having A Baby* was going to be up against such a popular programme. It was, Davina said, the worst slot.

Bad slot or not, by November, and now with the *Big Brother 6* saga and the flop of *He's Having A Baby* behind her, Davina took off to Africa, where, in four extraordinary days, she went from joy to despair and humility. She had gone there because she wanted to see first-hand how Comic Relief was working and to discover how, among other things, the charity was helping to improve the lives of a woman and her 10 grandchildren and how they had moved from a one-room accommodation to a larger home. With horror, she witnessed the desperation of children orphaned by AIDS at Africa's biggest slum. This was where she only just survived an attack by a swarm of bees, too. She hoped the diary she kept during her visit would help others understand what still needed to be done and, at the same time, share with others how her visit to Kenya was also one of her biggest life-changing experiences.

'Monday 10.15pm: I've just arrived in Kenya. It's my third visit to the country for Comic Relief and I've been asked to keep a diary detailing what happens. I always find writing diaries quite hard – there are so many things I want to say and feelings I want to convey, but when I put pen to paper somehow it never comes out right. I'll do my best.

'The first day has been tough. I felt nervous, unsure about what to expect from the slums this time. I remember my visits before, how horrific the living conditions and the sanitation levels were, and the claustrophobic feel of the small spaces in which people live. I really hoped there'd been some positive change, but it was shocking. The smell was indescribable and everywhere we walked there were open sewers in the streets.

'There was some hope, though. We met Wanjiru Macharia, who lives in the slums. She is part of The National Cooperative Housing Union (NACHU), a local organisation funded by Comic Relief, which helps people move from the slums into their very own basic, simple, precious home. They also get a small plot of land on which to grow vegetables, rear livestock and start to support themselves; it's an amazing thing.

'I was here to help Wanjiru and her family move out of the slums into a new settlement. She is now 70 and had three children: one daughter and two sons. Her daughter, who had 10 children, died of AIDS and Wanjiru was left to look after her grandchildren. She now has great-grandchildren, too. They currently sleep in one room huddled together on the floor with no running water and none of the comforts we take for granted.

'We helped Wanjiru load her belongings into a truck – just a bundle of clothes and a couple of bits of furniture. It was really moving to see how little she had. As Wanjiru prepared to leave, a big group of people gathered and started to sing a traditional African song to send her off. The atmosphere was incredible. It was clear everyone was happy for her to be escaping life in the slums, but I wondered how many were sad that they weren't leaving, too.

'We drove to Ruai, 40 minutes away, where Wanjiru

and her family would begin their new life. We saw the smiles spread across their faces as they settled into their new house with their own plot of land. In the slums the families are in constant fear of eviction as they are essentially squatting on government land.

'Back at the hotel, as I got ready for bed after an eventful day, I thought about Wanjiru and her family spending their first night in a proper house.

'Tuesday 7.15pm: I felt lonely this morning. Because of the time difference, I can't speak to my girls. Even when I'm surrounded by people I feel as if a part of me is missing.

'At 8am we all got into our cars and drove to Kibera, a slum in Nairobi. It's an horrific place with a population of 700,000, making it the biggest slum in the whole of Africa. It just seems to go on and on for miles. HIV and Aids are rife in Africa, wiping out a whole generation. Millions of grandmothers are having to bring up their grandchildren and great-grandchildren.

'As I was walking around, looking at all the children, they shouted out, "How are you? How are you?", which is the first English phrase they learn in school. I wondered how many of them are orphans. Someone once asked me what my greatest fear was and I said, "Dying before my children are old enough to look after themselves." I thought about this today, about how awful a mother must feel if she is really ill and has little babies.

'It must be frightening to know that your babies are going to be all alone in the world and living in desperate poverty. Every year more than 10 million children die of hunger and preventable diseases – that's one every three seconds. I leave feeling depressed; I just want to hold my girls.

'Wednesday 10.20pm: Wow, what an insane day! We got up early, were out of the hotel by 7.30am and at the airfield by 8.30am. We then flew to Maralal in Northern Kenya. When we arrived lots of the Samburu people who live in this region had come to see what the fuss was about. Two young girls stood together watching our every move, wearing the most amazing array of beads around their necks.

'After a 45-minute drive on a very rough dirt track we arrived at Baawa. All I could see was a sea of Samburu men in their finery. We were immediately taken to John's house, the Samburu tribesman we were going to be spending time with. John was in the middle of harvesting the honey from his bees, the sale of which provides his main source of income.

'Comic Relief, through a project called Resource Projects Kenya (RPK), has funded new hives, suits and proper smokers, which have helped reduce the huge risk of forest fires and made the hives more productive. John now makes enough money to send his kids to school.

'We waited until early evening to smoke out the bees because this was when they are meant to be sleepy and therefore less vicious, but they were everywhere and not quite as dopey as I had hoped. Suddenly one hit my face. I panicked and thought it had got inside my protective hat.

'I ran and ran, pulling off my hat, but the bee was caught in my hair. Someone caught up with me and got it out. I was so relieved, but it freaked me out and I imagined what it must have been like before the Samburu had their suits.

'Thursday 9.50pm: Today was so special. It's been such an honour to have been allowed to meet the Samburu people. We spent the day filming Nomargygi, a widow who had four children, although only one is still alive today. It was difficult for her to talk about her loss. Her face was furrowed with grief and she couldn't look at me.

'She lost her three children around the time of a fierce drought in 2000. At that time all the tribes people with herds left the villages to search for water for their animals so she was left alone with her four children. Three of them fell desperately ill but there was no one around to help her, so she could only watch as they all died.

'My heart ached as she told me the story. She showed me her house, made from mud and cedar posts. It was almost too big for her and her son – the empty beds must be a constant reminder of her horrific loss.

'The Samburu people gave us a good send-off and I was overcome. The last few days have been filled with so many emotions – anticipation, joy, despair and humility. Some of it has been difficult, but all of it has been amazing and I really feel as if I've learned something about my own life.'

13

SITTING PRETTY

If Davina had been asked in 1992 what she would like to be doing 15 years later, she would have probably said, 'Carry on what I'm doing now and keep a roof over my head.' In fact, that is exactly what she told her agent when he asked her the same question: 'My job is beyond my wildest dreams. I never imagined I'd be here now; I still get excited when I walk through the doors of the BBC.' Even sitting outside Television Centre with her father in a car, she still can't help but scream and shout, 'It's the BBC!'

And probably that's what she was doing in December 2005 when she had arrived at the Wood Lane studios, now as famous as EMI's Abbey Road, to film a pilot episode of her very own chat show.

Simply titled *Davina*, the show began its eight-week run two months later, on the evening after Valentine's Day, after which it was on for another seven weeks, every Wednesday night at 8pm. The news that Davina was being groomed as the first lady of prime-time chat had already hit the headlines the previous October. Among others, the *Daily Star* reported that she had already signed a £1 million deal to host a pre-watershed talk show, interviewing guests from the worlds of film, television and showbusiness. In doing so, she would be the first presenter of an early-evening weekday chat show since Terry Wogan's ended 14 years earlier.

The hope, as far as the BBC was concerned, was that she would be a smash hit. But was there really any reason why she wouldn't be? After all, she wasn't about to be pitched into everyone's home in the same risqué light as perhaps Jonathan Ross is. And on top of that, of course, there was the added bonus that she would attract legions of female fans to the channel. It was on 6 December 2005, soon after the not-for-broadcast pilot episode was recorded with guests – comedian Peter Kay, singer Charlotte Church and *EastEnders* actor Nigel Harman – under the watchful eye of former *Parkinson* producer Bea Ballard, that the series of eight shows was commissioned. At the time, a BBC spokeswoman agreed that, yes, 'Davina is a great choice because she has real energy and empathy, and she knows how to put people at ease. If anyone was going to be the BBC's first female prime-time chat show host, she's the one.'

It is perhaps interesting to ask why, if the BBC was trying to make viewers forget about *Parkinson*, did the show follow exactly the same format with a similar set? Only for Davina it was furbished in pink, with pink-cupped chairs, a coffee table to match, and her name as big as the set designers could build it in pink neon lights. Like *Parkinson*, *Davina* would feature interviews with three or four celebrities plus live music in the studio. Again, another small difference was that not all the guests would remain on set with any of the others, which, of course, on *Parkinson* they did. But it did follow what was pretty much the same format for every chat show. From *Wogan* to the *Jonathan Ross Show*, they all combine the same pattern.

Not that Davina's show would be seen as an immediate threat to Jonathan Ross's position as BBC1's main chat-show host. According to the article in the *Star*, a senior BBC source said, 'Our audience research tells us that Davina is particularly popular among women. She has the edgier aspect which comes from her work on *Big Brother* and from the fact she's lived a proper life; a lot of women think they can relate to her and they regard her as someone human rather than a showbiz floozy.' But offering up some contradiction for a journalist's chin-wag and serious debate was Davina's own comment from earlier the previous year when she reportedly said, 'I couldn't imagine doing what, say, Parky does – I'm more from the school of Oprah and Trisha.'

Two months later, on 7 December, the *Daily Mail* reported much the same as the *Star*, but now with more detailed information than had previously been known about Davina's new project, which, for some reason, the BBC was still keeping under wraps to a certain extent. In his article, the *Mail*'s media editor Matt Born also questioned whether Davina would prove a controversial choice. 'Despite widespread acclaim for fronting **Big Brother**, her loud and energetic style appears to irritate as many people as it entertains and, let us not forget, she was once included among a poll of 100 Worst Britons.' He went on to draw attention to Davina's mixed success in branching out into new programmes, highlighting her most recent ratings disaster, the Saturday-night show *He's Having A Baby* (eventually the programme was pulled). Peter Fincham, head of BBC1, remained unconcerned, saying, 'Her relationship with audiences is very special – viewers really like her.' The BBC hadn't had a chat show in peak time since Michael

Parkinson and Fincham was keen to point out that 'the fact that it's not being hosted by a man also makes it quite exciting.'

But as the *Mail* said, 'Whether Parkinson himself will welcome the comparison is debatable. The 70-year-old TV veteran has never disguised his contempt for the young pretenders to his chat-show crown, saying they were more interested in showing off than engaging with guests.'

Davina, however, did not entirely agree with all that was being bandied around the press. For a start, 'I'm not earning a million a year from the BBC – I have no contract. I'm just doing eight shows to start with.' Like anyone taking on a new challenge, especially in television, she realised some people would be gunning for her, while others would hate what she was setting out to do. As she admitted, 'I'm doing all right, so I'm easy to knock. Some probably think I'm a strong character and may find that alarming. I don't have a thick skin, so my motto is "don't read critics" – I'll have to prove them wrong. It will be a lot of fun, laughter and emotion.' Despite this, people persisted in calling her 'the new Parky', a description which filled her with horror. 'Even though I do partly want to be like Parky because he's bloody brilliant but, if I try to be like Parky, it's just going to seem weird, and I don't really know how I'm going to be, but it will be me.'

According to all those who have met Davina, know her or have worked with her, in person she is apparently softer looking and more delicate, oddly more reminiscent of the actress Dervla Kirwan than her own high-octane TV self. She has glossy hair that flops in her eyes, good teeth and cheekbones, no make-up. There is something endearing about her open quality. Her gaze is so steady and attentive that, if you commented on it, her explanation would be that perhaps it is because she has a slightly lazy eye. And there is, say most, a childlike aspect to her that belies her streetwise past and still clings to her without any suggestion that she is simple-minded. So why should she have been worried about the new direction of presenting towards which she was now heading and, at the same time, perhaps, moving away from the 'yoof' TV presenter bracket of which she had been queen for so long?

If she had one thing on her side to make her chat show successful, then it would probably be her colourful past and background. That alone would give her all the empathy she needed for emotionally needy interviewees. 'I've lived a lot, so I'll be able to say, "Been there. Done that." When I hear about friends who have relapsed and died, I'm very grateful to be around. Every day is borrowed time. Sure,' she continues, 'I could flirt with George Clooney and get something different. I'll tap his knee and ask how big his willy is – *joking*! I'll talk to a girl about make-up whereas Michael Parkinson can flirt with a woman or get matey about football. I feel his natural place is on the BBC, and it's odd to see him with ad breaks. I'm loath to say anything negative because he's TV royalty, and there are enough people slagging us off without us doing it to each other. I can't be Parky, or anything but me. I don't think I'll strip – done that, nothing to prove.'

All the same, Caitlin Moran of *The Times Online* questioned how Davina as a chat-show host would be received. 'I love Davina – who doesn't? As my gay friend Jimmy puts it, "She's a brassy bitch in classy boots – what's not to love?" But as McCall's previous interviewing experience is restricted to chatting with former inmates of *Big Brother*, one does wonder how this "fast-paced show full of glitz, glamour and gossip" will fare. Davina's post-eviction interviews were, after all, legendarily awful. And, if a woman can't get some satisfactory chit-chat out of George Galloway, realising that he will possibly never be able to gain paid employment again in the wake of pretending to be a sexy cat, then how's she going to ramp up the excitement with, say, James Blunt's new single?'

Another online critic, Steve Pratt, agreed. 'Davina may be taking a big risk in launching a new chat show.

Its peak-time slot means it has lots of competition and – she's a woman. Any new chat show is a risk and one placed in an eight o'clock prime-time slot is riskier than most.' The usual slot for chat shows is early evening or late night, so Davina needed to persuade viewers to transfer their affections from such programmes as the long-running police series *The Bill*, property show *Relocation Relocation*, *Live UEFA Cup Football* and even the *Winter Olympics* on the other main channels.

Having suffered a flop with BBC1's *He's Having A Baby*, she would have her work cut out. Not only this but in the British chat-show world she was a rarity, unlike the US, where Oprah Winfrey remains Queen of TV Talk.

Announcing her signing, BBC1 Controller Peter Fincham admitted, 'There aren't many chat shows with hosts that are women and this is very exciting for us. Since Michael Parkinson left, we haven't had a chat show before the news that's in peak time. We think that's a rather exciting thing to do; it's an exciting chat show that isn't hosted by a man. I think Davina is rather special and viewers really like her. I'm really glad she's here.'

Critic Steve Pratt went on to argue, 'But let a woman be in charge on her own? You've more chance of finding a happy marriage on a soap! Liking McCall as the presenter of C4's *Big Brother* is one thing, wanting to watch her own entertainment show featuring guests and live music is quite another thing.' In the past women have presented British chat shows but rarely as themselves. Caroline Aherne may have played at Mrs Merton, but Dame Edna Everage was hardly typical. For some reason Nigella Lawson didn't manage to pull of her mix of chat and cookery on ITV1's afternoon slot, but pairing with a man (Des and Mel, or Richard and Judy, for example) is a successful formula. It was also acceptable for Sue Lawley to sit in for Terry Wogan from time to time.

But Davina understood the challenge that lay ahead and that some people would be out to get her, whatever happened. Somehow she would need to attract decent guests and already she was being criticised for the opening show's lack of big names: 'Charlotte Church has done the talk-show circuit so much you may feel she has nothing left to say. Celebrity couple Vernon Kay and Tess Daly are hardly Burton and Taylor. And actor Max Beesley's appearance may not be entirely unconnected with his current BBC1 series *Hotel Babylon*.'

She realised too that many celebrities would wait to see how the first shows were received before offering themselves up for interview. Of course she already had experience in dealing with difficult guests, having debriefed a mixed bag of *Big Brother* housemates after their eviction. Davina could also claim to have interviewed everyone from transsexuals to MPs. Fortunately for her Parkinson's ITV show was off air as hers was about to begin. This meant she had a clear run at whichever Hollywood star happened to be in town; also the majority of the remaining competition had disappeared with Michael Aspel, Clive Anderson, Terry Wogan and Frank Skinner no longer doing chat shows.

Summing up, critic Steve Pratt at least offered her a few nuggets of encouragement, saying, 'With Parky looking increasingly past it, she might do well to follow the example of another BBC1 chat-show host, Jonathan Ross, or Paul O'Grady, whose ITV1 show won prizes, big audiences and a lucrative offer to move to C4. They're as much the stars of the show as their guests. The balance between promoting yourself and letting your visitors have their say is a tricky one. If McCall imposes her personality on the show, she might just pull it off. One day, like Oprah, she could have an A-list guest like Tom Cruise jumping up and down on her sofa declaring his love for his girlfriend.'

Despite what journalists like Moran and Pratt were predicting, Davina was realistic enough to realise, and even almost agree with Pratt, that not every interview could be, as she calls it, 'a corker'. It isn't for any interviewer. But all she needed, she was convinced, was three or four good guests a show. The only problem with that was that there weren't that many good ones around – and the ones that were, would they be available? 'A lot will hold back till they've seen the first shows. I'll have to prove myself. I hope I'll be amazing and guests will be knocking on my door. I have to think it's going to be great. If I thought I might be rubbish, I'd be on a losing streak.'

Not that 'losing streak' would have been the words to describe the first show when it was broadcast on 15 February 2006. Recorded on the Tuesday of the previous week, as is the case with most shows that supposedly go out live, or, on some occasions, a day or two before, apart from Charlotte Church, the line-up of guests had changed from the guest list of the pilot show. With Nigel Harman and Peter Kay missing, their places were taken by husband and wife presenters Tess Daly and Vernon Kay, who at the time were the 'It' couple from Bruce Forsyth's *Strictly Come Dancing*. Also appearing were heart-throb actor Max Beesley, best known for his role in *Hotel Babylon* opposite Tamsin Outhwaite, Davina's neighbour, Julian Clary and music from KT Tunstall.

Although Davina was raving about all her guests, she was particularly pleased to have Charlotte Church on the show. Apart from singing her then newest single 'Moodswings', and claiming she could karaoke any Girls Aloud song better than the girls themselves probably could, Church talked about her life with Welsh rugby union international Gavin Henson, singing and how proud she is to have given up smoking. 'I've always lived with Gav – three months into our relationship I just moved in. Now we've got our own place and I decorated it all. I didn't get any interior designers in – my dad did it all for me. In my bedroom I have got an Indian theme with all beautiful saris. It's got lots of dark wood, too, so it's not too girly. There were lots of stories in the press saying that Gavin really wanted me to give up smoking but he's not like that at all. Gavin never puts any pressure on me to be healthy or anything even though he's super healthy. He's a dreamboat; he's naturally gorgeous – he doesn't spend hours doing his hair or anything.'

One of the names Davina probably wouldn't turn down in the future would be Denzel Washington. 'I interviewed him once in a car, and fancied him a little, which isn't good because I can't think what I'm saying except "Gosh, you're lovely". I was like an over-excited puppy, but he stopped me after the first question to ask if I was nervous and then told me to pull down the window and scream. So I did. I felt so much better afterwards. But you can't interview properly if you're a fan, although deep admiration is different – which I have for Sir Ian McKellen – it is all right so long as you don't end up kissing his bottom. I don't mean in a gay way, but being too nice to him. I like to think that if I totally adored someone who needed challenging I'd do it, but not in a mean way. I'd like to build enough trust so you can ask tricky questions, like Oprah Winfrey.'

Among those on her wish list already were Dawn French, Kate Bush, Jordan, Bill Clinton and former *Big Brother* contestant Jade Goody – 'She's my favourite celebrity, who has done nothing to be famous for, but is genuinely loveable.'

As much as she had a wish list, she also had a definite no-no list as well. And one of those on that list was actress Shirley MacLaine. She was the first person Davina had interviewed on television and was, in her own words, such a cow. 'She crossed her arms, huffed and tutted, and I laughed because I thought she was joking, but she wasn't. Eventually she said, "Hold on a minute, honey, I'm trying to get over your questions." Afterwards, I cried and cried because she'd freaked me out. There wasn't one jot of warmth in her body – I think she hated me.'

It's funny, she continued, 'but my grandmother tries to get me to do something more gritty than a chat show, but it's important to entertain people. Tony

Blair probably doesn't want to watch Paxman or Andrew Marr. He'd prefer to kick off his shoes and see me. I'll try to be good, listen and not shout. If you're hooked on someone, it's easy to get a conversation going – I call it the force.' Even if her grandmother wasn't too keen on the whole idea, says Davina, 'she is amazing. Highly emotional, highly opinionated, very fair and moral and just, incredibly thoughtful and kind to the community she lives in. She does a lot of charity work, and she has a very strong faith and goes to church, and she used to say prayers to me every night. I mean, she's really... well, she's still the backbone of our family.'

It was on the day before Davina's show was broadcast that the *Mirror* was quick to report that she had already told friends she was expecting her third baby. Apparently, four or five days before her chat show, an excited Davina had broken the news at a party and had told pals she and husband Matthew Robertson were thrilled. She said, 'I'm expecting another baby and we're absolutely delighted; I'm so looking forward to having another baby. We are over the moon.'

One partygoer said, 'She was ecstatic – it was as if she had just been told she'd won a lottery rollover jackpot. I've seldom seen anyone so delirious with joy.'

Davina, who hid any sign of a bump under a heavy

coat as she left the BBC studios in London recently, said she would love to give Matthew a son.

She has claimed giving birth gave her a far bigger high than any drug she had ever tried. She said, 'My deliveries were orgasmic – they knocked spots off any drug. When those babies came out, I wanted to stand naked on the highest mountain and scream with pride. I could do it over again and again, and again.' She also admitted to feeling guilty about working because it meant she missed time with her family. Davina announced her baby news at friend Mark Diggin's 50th birthday party in Aviemore, Scotland.

But it wasn't all good news. In a posting made on *Low Culture*, a website that claims to refer to a wide variety of cultural themes characterised by their consumption by the masses, things weren't looking too bright. 'In 2002, long before we'd decided we wanted to work in television, we were answering some essay questions in the hope of being invited to attend a television festival in Edinburgh. One of the questions asked us was who we'd get to present a new chat show. We chose Davina McCall, because of what we considered her infectious warmth and her ability to get the best of her subjects on *Big Brother*. We feel that we should point out that we wrote this back when *Big Brother* was a mere two years old, when Davina was still sympathetic to the evictees rather than stitching them up in front of a baying mob every Friday, and of course back before she started shouting into the camera *all the damn time.*

'We're consulting our lawyers as to whether we have any kind of intellectual copyright on this idea, but in the meantime we thought we'd point out that Davina McCall will be hosting a new chat show on BBC1 tonight. It'll be interesting to see if she pulls this off, as there is a shortage of chat shows on terrestrial TV led by female presenters; Parky and Jonathan Ross seem to have the market sewn up. Davina's last effort for BBC1, the Saturday-night dad-fest *He's Having a Baby*, was something of a ratings low-point for the channel, so this is her chance to prove that it was the format and not the presenter at fault. The opening show will feature the ubiquitous Charlotte Church, who's usually fairly good value when encouraged to talk about virtually anything, along with Max Beesley and celebrity married couple Vernon Kay and Tess Daly. Of course, if it works, we'll be claiming credit for the idea all along, and if it all bombs we'll delete the first paragraph of this post and pretend that nothing every happened in true "these are not the droids you're looking for" style.'

And if it was true what was being said, post-broadcast, then, yes, that first paragraph was destined for the recycling bin because, according to the *Sun,*

Davina's new show got off to a very shaky start, pulling in just 3.5 million viewers. 'The *Big Brother* presenter's BBC1 slot got only half the audience of ITV1 rival *The Bill* when it launched at 8pm on Wednesday. The show was intended to put some sparkle back into the midweek line-up. But it flopped with less than 15 per cent of the TV audience tuning in. It was even beaten by Channel 4's *Relocation, Relocation* – which was watched by 3.7 million. But the *Winter Olympics* on BBC2 nearly matched it with 2.9 million viewers.' All the same, wasn't it slightly early to pass judgement after just one show had been done and dusted?

14

TO BE CONTINUED

When Davina turns up for a photo shoot for a January 2006 feature in *Red* magazine, as if confirming what most have said about her, she stops on the stairs of the studio to hug all and sundry, showing off her new winter coat, a pair of skintight 'Seven' jeans atop a pair of vertigo-inducing Dolce & Gabanna ankle boots. She looks great – well, yes, but she also looks as you would expect Davina to look.

Not long after her arrival, she's in the make-up chair ready for the day's transformation and settling down for a chat about hair, make-up, bodies and fashion with her long-time friend and confidante Jackie Clune. This is perhaps a bit strange to Clune as normally when they get together they discuss other things like parenting, relationships, sex and politics. But, for the *Red* interview, she is in full siren mode in celebration of her fantastic new body and her new fitness DVD, the second one released in her career.

Although she loved dressing up and wearing dresses, and on this occasion a £4,200 Jasper Conran made to order, she was still happier in comfy clothes. 'And unless I'm going out, I never wear heels.' She did much the same with make-up. 'I rarely wear it. When I have it done, I can only sit still for 45 minutes before I get antsy. If I'm doing it myself, I have one look and I never experiment, I've literally got one blusher, which I use on my eyes as well.'

If Davina's make-up hadn't changed since the 1980s, her body certainly had. Post-baby number two saw her reveal a perfectly toned and trim body. 'The only way I can lose weight is by doing exercise and dieting. If I do an hour of exercise three times a week, I can kind of eat normally.' And her then latest fitness DVD, *My Three 30 Minute Workouts*, shows just how she did it without any tricks or fads, just pure hard old-fashioned work with her two personal trainers. It was released amid a plethora of other celebrity fitness workout DVDs that had swamped superstore shelves the previous Christmas, featuring everyone imaginable from Jordan to *Coronation Street's* Debra Stephenson. Despite often feeling exhausted from her hectic work schedule and the demands of family life, Davina still swears she has never ducked out of a session. She kept it up because she didn't want to falter with her routine. But yes, she admits, like everybody, she has days when she doesn't feel like doing anything, and especially not a workout.

'This new DVD is genius because it's only half an hour, which is really do-able. But you have to do all the core strength moves slowly and give it your utmost. And the best thing about it is that you can turn us off. So there's an option on it. I used to watch Cindy Crawford's workout video, and she had Radu, her personal trainer, and he used to go "arms up and den and den breed out" and, after 76 times working out with it, it's like *"SHUT UP, RADU!"* But you can turn us off and listen to the music.'

Less than one month after the *Red* magazine photo shoot and interview, with Davina staring out from the cover and the quote 'I'm insecure like everyone else' sitting underneath her name, Davina was back on our screens with *Big Brother*, the show that is still the one with which most people associate her. If she still has moments of self-doubt, she explains them away by saying, yes, 'I get insecure like everyone else. I feel like a fat wreck when I'm pregnant – I hated it both times. I put on an extraordinary amount of weight and I was convinced Matthew was going to run off with someone else. You know, I have to admit that, when Traci Bingham walked into the *Big Brother* house, I was like, "OMIGOD, look at her!" And there was a part of me that hated her because she's beautiful, and she's got such a bodacious body and enormous boobs.'

Eventually, though, Davina did warm to Bingham during her time on the show because, as Davina would put it, she was just a really kind person who wanted to feel loved. 'With celebrities there's an element of people-pleasing and Traci is definitely one of these people and that's what makes watching her so painful because all she wants is to be loved and hugged, and appreciated and told she's beautiful.'

So would she ever have plastic surgery to get the Bingham babe look? one wonders. 'Well, I might have a boob job at 40 and I'm not averse to having a "freshen up" in my fifties. Having said that, I'm an addict so I'd have to be pretty careful – I could look like the Bride of Wildenstein quite quickly.' And it's hard to imagine Davina with a Jordan-type chest or even a chest like Winona Ryder's, who, according to former lover and Jamiroquai frontman Jay Kay, 'has these enormous breasts, bigger than they look on film'.

What was it that Davina still loves about *Big Brother*? 'Well,' she says, without hesitation, 'it's when contestants say that they've learned something about themselves from the experience. Because for some of them it is a journey, a very personal one, and being in that house makes you look at yourself. I mean, you've got nothing else to do except think about yourself and how your behaviour affects other people, and how their behaviour affects you and how when there's an argument you have to resolve it or else it just goes on and on. And it's having to deal with things and deal with them in an open way and do stuff that you'd never normally do on the outside.'

Nadia, the transsexual who emerged winner of *Big Brother 5* in 2004, was one of Davina's favourites. That was the series that got most people in the country hooked. Following Nadia over the weeks sometimes felt like watching an Almodóvar film which turned into *The Elephant Man* in that extraordinary moment when she broke down in front of the camera and sobbed, 'I am... not... a man.'

As Davina says, 'There was real emotion there. She wasn't in it for the money. I really believe she was in it for recognition and affection, and that was an incredibly powerful and beautiful thing.'

Looking back at that series, it was trailed as '*Big Brother* turns evil', and, from the start, it did appear to be controversial. To begin with, the house was much smaller than previous editions and far more claustrophobic. There was one bedroom, and the prize money of £100,000 was reduced if housemates failed to complete their tasks. Not only that but *Big Brother* promised tougher challenges as well as surprises to test the minds of the housemates. What's more, the makers were initially criticised for choosing contestants specifically to boost ratings, opting for people who were openly gay: Marco and Dan, transsexual Nadia Almada, a former asylum seeker Ahmed, and Jason, who claimed to be bisexual, although he later revealed that this had been nothing more than fabrication on his part, simply to improve his chances of being selected for the programme. And, once he got on it, his feeling of being attracted and willing to either sex soon dissipated to a large extent as the personalities of the housemates overshadowed the issues he thought he may have had.

Generally, the housemates were all strong opinionated characters. Kitten Pinder was evicted in the first week for constant rule-breaking. A fake eviction in the second week saw two of the housemates, Emma and Michelle, confined to the nearby '*Big Brother* bedsit', where they could see and hear what was happening in the house without the others knowing. After their return to the house, scenes of aggression and near-violence erupted, resulting in on-site security staff having to enter the house for the first time in the show's history. Some viewers of the live feed also called the police. After a short investigation, a joint statement by Hertfordshire Police and producers Endemol said that they were satisfied with steps being taken to ensure the safety and well-being of the housemates. Police also reportedly questioned each contestant as they left the house. Emma was moved back to the bedsit and later evicted permanently. A psychologist on the show resigned, claiming his warnings that Endemol's deliberate selection of housemates was likely to cause conflict and would lead to the disruption and the fight that it did went unheeded.

After the fight, further arguments broke out and several housemates received formal warnings from *Big Brother*, but nothing on the scale of what producers refer to as 'Day 20' or 'Fight Night'. Following an appearance on MTV's *Total Request Live*, Emma and Victor clashed again and had to be separated by the security on the show.

A surprise new housemate, Becki Seddiki, was evicted at the first opportunity. She had been told by *Big Brother*, based on first impressions, to kiss one of the housemates and that housemate would be up for eviction. This became known as the 'Judas kiss'. She chose Michelle, which proved a highly unpopular choice, and this is probably the reason for her eviction. The weekly live task was dropped; however, housemates still competed in a 'Saturday Challenge', but only highlights were shown. The week after Seddiki's eviction, Ahmed Aghil was evicted. And, the following week, the flamboyant, aggressive Victor Ebuwa left the house. The week after that, Michelle Bass was the choice for eviction.

Overall, the series was notable for Michelle's romance with Stuart Wilson. It is widely believed that they were the first couple to have full sex on the main *Big Brother* UK show (this having already taken place on *Teen Big Brother* in 2003), following two incidents where they made a crude tent and discarded their microphones. However, their actions were not visible, and both parties have refused to confirm or deny what may or may not have gone on. Michelle's self-confessed jealous behaviour gave some viewers the impression that Stuart was an unwilling participant in the affair, but he has since stated that this was not the case. The relationship continued after both had left the house.

Two days before the final day, Stuart Wilson received only 7 per cent of the votes to win, the lowest amount of the contestants in the house, and so he was evicted. All five remaining housemates were enjoying a party for winning a mini task when he was called into the Diary Room. Stuart was then told he was to leave immediately, without saying goodbye to the remaining housemates. He was very enthusiastic and well received on leaving the *Big Brother* house. Nadia, as expected by all the bookmakers, won *Big Brother 5* with 74 per cent of the vote. She was greeted by an adoring crowd, who chanted her name.

Big Brother 5 was also notable for the introduction by two of the housemates of the eviction pose, which led to several evictees doing poses during *Big Brother 6*. First, Victor struck a 'cool' pose in keeping with his house 'gangsta' persona, leaning against the wall sideways on to the waiting audience. Later, Dan, who could possibly have seen Victor before the inner doors closed, stood, head bowed, arms out, before lifting his head.

So with all that in mind, and always being prepared to expect the unexpected, what could be expected from the fourth *Celebrity Big Brother* that started its run of potential mayhem and chaos just five days after the New Year celebrations passed? Ten minutes into the launch show on 5 January 2006, most viewers must have got a pretty good idea what was in store as Davina shared the big secret with everyone who had tuned in. Almost beside herself with synthetic glee, she revealed that, while 10 celebrities would be entering the house, there would actually be 11 housemates that year. The first one in would be an ordinary member of the public who – and Davina paused again to relish the sheer wild invention of it all – 'has to pretend that they're famous!'

What neither Davina nor anyone else could have imagined was that the latest edition of *Celebrity Big Brother* would be won by a fake celebrity. Chantelle Houghton was a 23-year-old promotions girl from Essex. Before *Big Brother*, her only claim to fame was that she was a Paris Hilton lookalike. In the years to come, she will probably become more famous for having instant fame handed to her on a plate by being the first non-celebrity to win *Big Brother* in a celebrity series. As was more or less expected, her first task, once inside the *Big Brother* house, was to convince her celebrity housemates that she was actually a genuine celebrity. Failure to achieve this would have resulted in her eviction on Day 4. In the Diary Room, she was told that she was to role-play the character of a pop star from the fictitious girl band Kandy Floss and that her biggest hit was 'I Want It Right Now' – a song, interestingly enough, that had been penned with Kylie Minogue in mind. But as early as Day 2 viewers were already wondering if she had been found out when Preston of the Ordinary Boys band briefed George Galloway, Jodie Marsh and Faria Alam of his suspicion that Chantelle was a red herring. 'I've never heard of Kandy Floss, and I know about pop music.'

On the same day, Chantelle met one of her most difficult challenges. Each housemate had to take turns to show each other what they were famous for, or had been made famous by. Whereas Traci Bingham could do a slow-motion run as she had done every week in the opening credits of *Baywatch* when it was the most watched programme on television, Michael Barrymore could choose any one of a hundred comedy routines

and Pete Burns bowled everyone over with a chorus
from 'You Spin Me Right Round', the only thing
Chantelle could do was a verse or two from 'I Want It
Right Now', the fake hit her fake group was meant to
have had. The only problem was that she couldn't sing
a note, and had precious little time to learn the words
and melody. Armed with lyrics on a sheet of paper, she
just about managed to scrape her way through, not
that she looked very convincing or confident if you
consider that she was meant to be a famous member of
a famous girl band.

It was probably Chantelle's less than mediocre
performance that more or less convinced Preston that
she was indeed a red herring, not a real celebrity at all.
She was even faced with his tough interrogation when
he put it to her that he thought she had been sent in by
Big Brother. Although he didn't entirely admit to
thinking she was an impostor, he did say he was
suspicious because he had never heard of Kandy Floss
before. But Chantelle kept her calm and informed him
that he was completely wrong, and even took an oath
on her mother's life that she was the real deal.

But the real test was on Day 3 when, in nail-biting
television, all the celebrities had to place themselves in
order of fame on a fame chart. Luckily for Chantelle,
she was placed ninth, which meant she could stay in
and was able to announce to the others that she was

not, in fact, a celebrity. Of course, Chantelle's mission to stay in the house wasn't the only talking point of the series. There were many other highlights and probably the most remarkable one was when a coat owned by Pete Burns was taken from the *Big Brother* house by Hertfordshire Police after a series of complaints had been received that it may have been made from gorilla fur. It turned out that, although the coat fur was of monkey origin, it had not been imported illegally. Of course, it would have been more shocking had the suspicions been true. It would probably have meant that Burns could have faced up to five years in prison and an unlimited fine under the Convention on International Trade in Endangered Species.

Another extraordinary moment, as the *Mirror* pointed out, was when 'heartless Michael Barrymore shocked TV viewers with a "comedy" impersonation of Adolf Hitler. The out of favour entertainer chose the imitation of the hated Third Reich leader when *Big Brother* asked contestants to "give a performance based on what he was best known for in the outside world". Even host Davina McCall warned viewers they might want to turn away and housemates looked uneasy as Barrymore told them, "We'd like to take you back 40 years ago when the first *Big Brother* was on air and it was shown in Germany."

'He turned away from the camera to grease down

his hair and drew a moustache with boot polish. Pete Burns, Jodie Marsh, Preston and Dennis Rodman clearly didn't know what to make of it as Barrymore tried to squeeze out laughs with over-the-top gestures and Nazi salutes. A TV insider said, "It was totally bizarre. What a weird choice for a comedy act." Barrymore had already been rapped by *Big Brother* bosses for gouging the eyes out of a picture of the Queen.

'He also made Jodie Marsh cry after accusing her of being a bully, who was only interested in talking about herself. He told her, "If you're not talking about your life, you shut down." Shocked Jodie branded his attack "offensive" and argued, "I talk about a lot of things." Before bursting into tears, she added, "I don't bully." She said she was low because it was the third anniversary of best friend Kim Banyard, who was strangled and bludgeoned in 2003 on her 22nd birthday by boyfriend Jonathan Dore. The couple's baby, Jake, was then only 10 weeks old. Dore, who strangled Kim at home in Pitsea, Essex, was jailed for life. A TV insider said, "It is an extremely hard time for Jodie. The anniversary will bring it all back. She could completely fall to pieces."'

Certainly, Jodie's 'falling to pieces' seemed to be high on the highlight list. She was about the only person who had been seen on a *Celebrity Big Brother* who, when advised that she might want to calm down at the risk of alienating the voting public, had sobbed, 'Wooooaaaaargh! I might as well *KILL MYSELF!*' and burst into a deafening flood of insane tears.

As one journalist noted, 'I suppose we should feel a little bit sorry for Jodie, as this must surely be the end of her career in the public eye. But, when someone goes on to *Celebrity Big Brother* – as she did – wanting to show the country the real Jodie Marsh, only for the real Jodie Marsh to turn out to be infinitely more pathetic, shallow, fragile and mental than the Jodie Marsh we knew from the newspapers, most probably all viewers, and maybe Davina too, couldn't help but feel that she deserves to leave the house.' Perhaps that's why she was the first one evicted.

But her drama-queen antics didn't stop there, agreed most reports. On the night of her eviction, Jodie's interview with Davina was much the same. That's when she blasted housemates for making her stay 'hideous'. The glamour model, sexpert, anti-bullying campaigner and arch-enemy of fellow glamour model Jordan defiantly slapped her backside as fans greeted her with boos and cheers. And she tore into Pete Burns and Michael Barrymore for being insensitively abusive to her. Fighting back her tears, she told Davina, 'It was so miserable in there. It was evil, hideous. I got so much stick – I was either miserable or defending myself.' She branded Burns 'the most hideous thing I've ever met. I wasn't sure how much longer I could sit and look at him. I defy anyone to be in there for three weeks and not want to kill themselves or him.'

As for Barrymore, she complained, 'He went on and on, and got on my case. In the end, when he blew at me, I thought, "He needs serious help."' Earlier, in the house, she had taken a bitter swipe at Barrymore over the March 2001 death of Stuart Lubbock in Barrymore's swimming pool, after they had clashed over putting meat on the shopping list. She told Chantelle, 'He's got a major issue with vegetarians. He keeps going on about it. Well, I've got an issue with people dying in pools but I don't keep on about it!' Jodie, who was up for nomination with Burns and George Galloway, was evicted with nearly 42 per cent of viewers' votes.

Perhaps it was because Barrymore had refused to speak publicly about the Lubbock incident and left Britain for a new life in New Zealand with his partner Shaun Davis that his return to television in the UK on *Celebrity Big Brother* incited a new attempt for a prosecution by the Lubbock family. Their lawyer, Tony Bennett, submitted legal papers to have Barrymore charged with drug offences and assault on 10 February 2006. In a statement, Barrymore said, 'I remain totally committed as I always have been to continue pursuing the truth about Stuart Lubbock's death on that tragic evening and would very much welcome working alongside Mr Terry Lubbock to uncover the truth. Allegations about drugs from that night have always been a complete irrelevance as to how Stuart Lubbock suffered those injuries. The court held that Mr Bennett's misguided application today to prosecute me for drug offences was an abuse of process, not in the public interest, and the evidence which he relied upon today was inadequate or unlawfully obtained.'

On learning she had been evicted from the *Big Brother* house, Marsh said, 'Thank you,' and hugged the housemates. She told fellow Essex girl Chantelle, 'Don't you dare cry – you'll set me off.' Outside she shouted, 'Where's my mum? Is my dog here?' and yelled, 'I love you!' as she spotted her family. She told Davina, 'The thing that kept me going every day was my friends and family. I hated the abuse; I got shouted at so many times in the house I couldn't bear it any more.' Many housemates had voiced outrage at her X-rated revelations, but Jodie hit back, 'In this day and age there's nothing wrong with a woman saying, "I like sex." That doesn't mean I sleep with every man I meet.'

She insisted that would include randy former basketball ace Dennis Rodman. 'He said he's never had a woman turn him down. Well, he's not going to have me.' But not all the housemates were in for a battering. She called Faria 'a good laugh and a top bird'. Her favourite, though, was Chantelle, whom she hoped would win.

Perhaps a surprise to everyone, on the same night, was the appearance of veteran DJ and entertainer Jimmy Savile, who stepped into the *Big Brother* house to grant one housemate one wish, just as he had helped make children's dreams come true for 20 years on the much-loved *Jim'll Fix It*. The housemate turned out to be Rodman, who, among other goodies, asked for a supply of cigarettes for all those housemates who were in desperate need to feed their habit.

And, of course, *Big Brother* wouldn't have been *Big Brother* without the possibility of some flirting, sex or romance. Certainly, observed most viewers, as well as the housemates, there was the unmistakable attraction between Preston and Chantelle. Even though there was no fondling each other or climbing into bed, or having sex on camera inside the house, it was one week after everyone had left the house that Preston declared his love for her in the *Sunday Mirror*: 'I lied to Davina – I *do* love Chantelle.' In the revelation he made to the tabloid, 'He admitted he is now desperately torn between his longing for the *Celebrity Big Brother* winner and girlfriend Camille Aznar, 25. Eight million viewers saw him come out of the *Big Brother* house and insist nothing was going on between them. Baring his soul to the *Sunday Mirror*, he revealed, "I'm sorry but I told a lie... I love Chantelle." He went on, "I love Camille and I want to do right by her. But now I also love Chantelle, and she's going to be in my life. It's messy, but the truth is I love them both." Ordinary Boys singer Preston, 24, told *Big Brother* host Davina McCall on Friday that he and Chantelle Houghton, 23, had no sexual connection.'

Overall, though, as *OK!* pointed out, 'Despite all their suffering, arguing and complaining during their time in the house, the celebrity housemates certainly gave us some truly magic moments. Claws came out in diva-style squabbles, gorilla fur flew, wigs were worn and skintight leotard dances were performed. After Dennis Rodman and George Galloway were evicted, six housemates remained in the grand final. As the housemates gathered on those yellow sofas, quaffing whatever remaining booze they had in the house, the atmosphere was so tense you could hear a pin drop as they waited for Davina McCall to announce the results.

'The first to be evicted was former *Baywatch* babe Traci "awesome" Bingham. She was followed by an unrepentant Pete Burns. Next to go was Ordinary Boys' frontman Preston, followed by Goldie Lookin Chain's Maggot. In second place was Michael Barrymore, but first place went to non-celebrity Chantelle Houghton. On her exit from the house, the bubbly blonde held her head, screaming "Oh my

God!" in disbelief and couldn't believe the paparazzi, the screaming public and explosive fireworks display awaiting her. "Davina, are you sure you've got this right?" she asked more than once.

'Some called her dim-witted, others called her Paris "Travelodge", but there's no denying Chantelle had the nation gripped. She charmed us with her sublime acting, infectious giggling, unforgettable singing and legendary Chantelle-isms.'

So that was three weeks of *Celebrity Big Brother 4*, and *The Times Online* correspondent, the Urban Fox, asked how could most of Britain stomach Davina McCall much longer? 'For the past few weeks, the Miss Whippy frontwoman of *Celebrity Big Brother* has been thrilling, if terrifying millions of us who have watched her interviewing the evicted inmates of the *Big Brother* house.'

The Urban Fox likened popular programming to gang mentality, in which presenter and audience got together to torment a victim, then went off to whisper together in a corner, picking over the pieces in the way of playground bullies. According to them, a new kind of 'not-quite-adult viciousness' was personified by Davina, who had apparently given Page Three girl Jodie Marsh and deflated George Galloway a 'kicking on their way back to reality.' While admitting to have awaited the arrival of *Big Brother* each night 'with all the twitchy eagerness of an addict craving a fix', the Urban Fox went on to describe the programme as being 'now mixed up in my mind with January's ugly news story of the "happy slapping" killing of a gay bar manager by a teenage gang led by a fourteen-year-old girl. Teenager Chelsea O'Mahoney told 37-year-old David Morley to "pose for the camera" before she took pictures on her mobile of her friends attacking him. Then she kicked him in the head herself. She and her three companions were acquitted of murder but convicted of manslaughter. "She kicked him like you would kick a football or rugby ball," recalled David Morley's friend, who was savagely beaten himself but escaped with his life, "just swinging her right foot back and kicking him really hard in the head."

Conceding no one had actually died on *Celebrity Big Brother* and the contestants were celebrities, who chose to be there and chose to display their stress and pain; also that it was hard to feel too sorry for some of the victims, the Urban Fox went on to say, 'The editing of events inside the house makes their viciousness seem unreal and cartoonish. No sooner have we joined forces to detest someone than they're brought low. First we're given permission to slaver over George Galloway's pop-eyed bullying of Michael Barrymore. Just hours later, we're complicit in Davina McCall's bullying of the evicted George Galloway.' Davina's power and the power of the medium of TV in general were brought into question, as was the viewers' role as arbiters of the victims' fate, 'What qualifies Davina McCall to teach them those harsh lessons on behalf of the public at large? And, if we suspect that even a few of the tears we've been treated to on screen are sincere, what are we doing getting such pleasure from watching?'

Perhaps it was a little unfair to compare Davina's stance on *Celebrity Big Brother* with that of Chelsea O'Mahoney. Judge Brian Barker was so appalled at the actions of the teenage bullies from Kennington that he lifted an order banning their identification as they were jailed for eight years, saying, 'No one listening to this case could fail to have been affected by your selfishness and blindness to the suffering of others. You sought enjoyment from humiliation and pleasure from the infliction of pain.' 'Pleasure from the infliction of pain' was a syndrome familiar to all *Big Brother* watchers reported the Urban Fox, who went on to remind us how Germaine Greer had walked out of an earlier round of the programme after five-and-a-half days. At the time she stated, 'Because I was being drawn into complicity with bullying, originally instigated by the production team, and slavishly followed by the housemates... I wasn't prepared to join in the persecution of any of these people, even if in retrospect I think they were callously indifferent to their own degradation.'

The Urban Fox went on to suggest that it might be as wrong to blame *Big Brother* as it was to blame George Galloway, and maybe the audience should turn on themselves for 'egging producers and presenter on to ever worse excesses because we, like Romans at the forum, can't wait for the lions to tuck in to their living dinner. When a *Big Brother* punter – I forget which – growled, "I'd like to smash your face in," the ugly truth is that we would all have wanted him to go ahead, just for the fun of it. A culture in which cruelty is so openly celebrated is one in which future Chelsea O'Mahoneys may not see the dividing line between professionally made bully TV and their own homemade violence videos.'

Sometimes, though, it doesn't matter what the critics think, and on this occasion it seemed that such petty snipes at one of the most popular shows on television were meaningless. All the same, there had been times in the past when Davina came rushing to the defence of the show. One of those times was in August 2005. That's when she told the *Radio Times* that the show's contestants represented a balance of British society and were not 'freaks'. The sixth series finale was watched by 7.7 million viewers, making it Channel 4's most popular show of the year.

'McCall said one of the only reasons she could think of for leaving is if producers started trying to manipulate people inside the house too much. She added that she was under no illusions that it was a difficult job to do. "It's easy to present – out with a very, very rowdy crowd talking to the camera. But somebody would find it hard to come and do it – a bit like trying to fill Cilla's shoes on *Blind Date*." McCall has an answer to the criticism that *Big Brother* routinely faces. "The people who go into that house are a cross section of British culture. They're not freaks. Most of the people who put *Big Brother* down are pseudo-intellectuals who have never really watched it. If you do, it's a fascinating insight into life."'

And, if any further proof were needed of the show's popularity, the day after Davina's chat show had aired, she made a special appearance at Madame Tussaud's. She unveiled a waxwork of herself and treated fans of the show to a first look at the new added attraction to the famous waxworks museum. For anyone dreaming of a place in the TV reality show, it was the next best thing. It was also where they could now get some practice in, if they ever did get selected.

When the '*Big Brother* Experience' first opened to the public on 16 February 2006, it came complete with a Diary Room for spilling out secrets and a 'talking' Davina wax double that was adorned in the same dress she wore on winner Nadia's eviction night in series 5. And the Diary Room was based on the one that featured in that same edition, and would, promised the publicity, give visitors the chance to share a live encounter with *Big Brother*.

Davina, of course, had recorded several sound-bites for her figure, and none more familiar than the one based on what she says on the show but just slightly modified for the waxwork: '*Big Brother* housemates, you are live at Madame Tussaud's. Please do not swear.'

The reality show had, by this time, become such a huge TV phenomenon, with 3 million people voting in the final of *Celebrity Big Brother*, that perhaps it is not surprising that Tussaud's had decided to include it among their newest attractions for 2006. On seeing her model for the first time, Davina was shocked. 'Oh my God, it's brilliant! It's even got my funny hand.' But, when asked about her pregnancy, news of which had just broken in several of the tabloids the day before, she had no comment and nor did her spokesperson. Well, not for the time being, at any rate. But, according to an onlooker at the unveiling ceremony, she clearly had children on her mind when she apparently made a beeline for a child who was at the attraction, who perhaps looked lost, and asked, as any concerned adult would, 'Is that someone's kid? He's gorgeous.'

With or without the waxwork, it would perhaps be easy for some to feel envious of Davina McCall's life in

2006. She is happily married to Matthew Robertson, now an outward bound instructor, and they have, by all accounts, two lovely daughters – 4-year-old Holly and 2-year-old Tilly – and with another reported to be on its way, what could be better? Davina, it seems, appears to have achieved most of her dreams by sheer force of will, something that a lot of people struggle for a lifetime to acquire. Above all, she says, 'I like working and being a mum, so it's a bit of a juggling act. It's not easy and I spend a lot of time feeling guilty. I'm imagining working less when the kids are teenagers. When I had children, that ambitious person that I was, the one who worked six days a week, 17 hours a days, disappeared. Now I want at least three or four days off a week so I can be with the kids.' Not that there is any long-term career plan or anything like that.

Although Davina is now heading towards 40 and is in the enviable position over and above such names as Victoria Beckham and Catherine Zeta Jones as the face of beauty giant Garnier, promoting their hair colours and creams (a position she achieved after research showed her to be the celebrity most British women wanted to be like), growing old doesn't seem to bother her either, or, if it does, then she doesn't let it show. And why should it when, as she says, 'I genuinely feel I am becoming more balanced the older I get. Reinvention is not necessarily about becoming a completely different person. With each year that you grow, you become a more evolved version of yourself.'

It's hard to define what she has, but, as her French mother might put it, Davina definitely has a certain *je ne sais quoi*. Today, she is routinely talked about in hyperbolic terms as one of the highest-paid female presenters, and, with the new BBC show and then, presumably, back to Channel 4 for the umpteenth series of domestic squabbles in the *Big Brother* house, that is probably true. 'I've been very, very blessed to have a corker of a show to always come back to and I don't know where my career would be if I didn't have *Big Brother*, but thank goodness I have.'

Perhaps it's because Davina has had more cause to examine herself than most of us, but she's rather good at assessing what makes her so popular. 'One thing I had in my favour is that I've never been skinny and I'm not putting myself down, but, although I think I'm attractive and I know what my good features are, I've never thought of myself as a stunning beauty. And that's a good thing for me because sometimes if you are really, really beautiful you're quite alienating.'

Even as she prepared herself for photographer David Gubert to shoot the photographs that ended up in *Red* magazine, she hooted, 'I'm on a bed, the sun is shining, I'm wearing thousands of pounds' worth of diamonds and everyone fancies me. Life's great!'

DAVINA McCALL'S TELEVISION

This listing of Davina's television shows relates only to programmes she has presented/hosted/co-hosted and does not include miscellaneous appearances. The data was compiled from information logged at the British Film Institute Library in London and from the Internet Movie Database (imdb.com).

2006 – *Big Brother 7*
2006 – *Davina*
2006 – *Celebrity Big Brother 4*
2005 – *He's Having A Baby*
2005 – *A Bear's Tail*
2005 – *The British Academy Television Awards*
2005 – *Celebrity Big Brother 3*
2005 – *Big Brother 6*
2004 – *A Bear's Christmas Tail*
2004 – *Love On A Saturday Night*
2004 – *Big Brother 5*
2003 – *Reborn In The USA*
2003 – *Big Brother 4*
2003 – *The Brit Awards*
2003 – *Stars In Their Eyes: Soap Stars Special*
2003 – *Stars In Their Eyes: Coronation Street Special*
2003 – *Stars In Their Eyes: Legends Special*
2002 – *Celebrity Big Brother 2*

2002 – *Popstars: The Rivals*
2002 – *The BAFTA Television Awards*
2002 – *Big Brother 3*
2002 – *The Vault*
2001 – *Oblivious*
2001 – *Big Brother 2*
2001 – *Sam's Game*
2001 – *Comic Relief Presents*
2001 – *Celebrity Big Brother*
2001 – *Don't Try This At Home*
2001 – *Streetmate*
2000 – *Don't Try This At Home*
2000 – *The Brit Awards*
2000 – *Big Brother 1*
2000 – *Don't Try This At Home*
1999 – *Birth Race 2000*
1999 – *Red Nose Day*
1999 – *This Morning*
1999 – *Don't Try This At Home*
1999 – *The Real Holiday Show*
1999 – *Streetmate*
1999 – *The Real Holiday Show*
1999 – *Prickly Heat*
1988 – *The Real Holiday Show*
1998 – *Streetmate*
1998 – *The Royal Tournament*
1998 – *Prickly Heat*

1998 – *Don't Try This At Home*
1998 – *This Morning*
1998 – *The Royal Tournament*
1997 – *House Hunters*
1997 – *Dream Ticket*
1997 – *Good Stuff*
1995 – *God's Gift*
1992 – *MTV's Most Wanted*

DAVINA McCALL'S AWARDS & NOMINATIONS

National Television Awards

2005
Most Popular Entertainment Presenter for *Big Brother*
Nominated

2004
Most Popular Entertainment Presenter
Nominated

2003
Most Popular Entertainment Presenter
Nominated

2002
Most Popular Entertainment Presenter
Nominated

2000
Most Popular Entertainment Presenter for
Don't Try This At Home
Nominated

RTS Television Awards

2002
Best Presenter for *Big Brother*
Nominated

TRIC Awards

2003
TV Personality
Winner